WELLINGTON

POCKET
GIANTS

GARY
SHEFFIELD

Cover image: Portrait of Arthur Wellesley, 1st Duke of Wellington by Thomas Lawrence in 1914. (English Heritage Photo Library)

Map illustrations by Thomas Bohm, User Design, Illustration and Typesetting

First published 2017

The History Press
The Mill, Brimscombe Port
Stroud, Gloucestershire, GL5 2QG
www.thehistorypress.co.uk

British Library Cataloguing in Publication Data.
A catalogue record for this book is available from the British Library.

ISBN 978 0 7509 5296 5

Typesetting and origination by The History Press
Printed and bound in Great Britain

Contents

1

A Fighting General

The 1st Duke of Wellington is one of the big beasts of British history. He was the most successful British general of the Revolutionary and Napoleonic Wars, and one of the finest British generals of all time, arguably *the* finest; and can be compared favourably with the greatest commanders from other countries and ages. His victories in the Peninsular War (1808–14) and Waterloo (1815) gave Britain immense international prestige, and helped lay the foundation for the century of British greatness that was to follow. From Waterloo until his death in 1852 Wellington was a dominating presence in British life. He was an important player on the political scene, having spells as Prime Minister during some of the most turbulent times in nineteenth-century British history. In his lifetime Wellington was a national hero, although not an uncontested one. Posthumously the controversies faded, and it was Wellington the soldier, not Wellington the controversial politician, that was remembered.

This book appears in a series on historical 'giants'. Wellington's claim to be a giant rests squarely on his career as a fighting general, which climaxed in 1815. His post-Waterloo career as a politician is not the pedestal upon which his greatness stands. So in keeping with the theme of the series, the focus is on Wellington the military commander, with his life after Waterloo being dealt with only briefly.

We are living though a golden age of scholarship on Wellington. Rory Muir's two-volume life, backed by an informative website, is an immensely impressive piece of scholarship. Huw Davies' military biography is likewise a substantial contribution to our understanding of Wellington. In addition to these books, a number of other important works have appeared in the last twenty years or so, by Bruce Collins, Charles Esdaile, Ian Fletcher, Alan Forrest, David Gates, Paddy Griffith, Christopher D. Hall, Philip Haythornthwaite, Richard Holmes, Donald Horward, Roger Knight, Joshua Moon and John Severn, among others. This has added to older but still useful books in the Wellingtonian canon by the likes of Anthony Brett-James, David Chandler, Godfrey Davies, John Fortescue, Michael Glover, Philip Guedalla, Elizabeth Longford, Charles Oman, S.P.G. Ward and Jac Weller. Why then do we need another book on Wellington? My first answer is that a very short book based on a synthesis of up-to-date scholarship and original sources fills a niche in the market. My second answer is that I wanted to write it.

I have been fascinated by Wellington since my early teens, when I read Elizabeth Longford's classic biography. Although my academic career has taken the path of a military historian of the twentieth century, my interest in the Napoleonic period has never left me. I have been fortunate enough to lead study tours to Waterloo, and to Wellington's battlefields in Spain and Portugal (not, alas,

India – or not yet anyway). The opportunity of writing a short biography proved too tempting to resist.

When I began to research this book, I wondered whether Wellington would, after all, turn out to be a giant. The reputations of historical figures are always ripe for revision, especially one who has been the subject of some fairly uncritical hagiography. And yet having written the book, having taken into account his mistakes, the large slices of luck that he enjoyed at critical points of his career, and the less-than-attractive facets of his personality, I have come to the conclusion that Wellington's reputation as a military commander is deserved. Wellington's contemporary, the great Prussian military theorist Karl von Clausewitz, wrote of individuals with 'appropriate gifts of intellect and temperament ... in a harmonious combination,' in possession of 'very highly developed mental aptitude for a particular occupation'.[1] Such people had 'genius'. One such, as this book argues, was the Duke of Wellington.

2

Irish Beginnings

Arthur Wellesley, 1st Duke of Wellington was born in Ireland. He was thus one of a long line of Irish soldiers, or at least soldiers with strong Irish connections, that have contributed much to the British army down the years. And yet the British army has always had an ambivalent relationship with Ireland. More than once British troops have been deployed on Irish soil to confront insurgency and outright rebellion, and Irishmen serving in the army were subject to suspicion about their loyalty to the Crown. This was particularly the case in Wellington's lifetime. He was the product of the Anglo-Irish Ascendancy: a caste of Protestant landowners, translated from the England and Scotland of centuries before, which held sway over a largely Roman Catholic and extremely poor population. Wellington always had something of the loner and outsider about him, and more than one biographer has seen his Ascendency background, as a member of a beleaguered, privileged minority in an alien land, as a key to his character. Tensions and repression in the Ireland of Wellington's youth certainly existed, but the idea that Arthur Wellesley was shaped by the insecurity of a settler class that constantly feared disaster at the hands of the colonised should not be overstressed. Ireland was simultaneously 'too physically close and too similar to Great Britain to be treated as a colony, but too separate and too different to be a region of the metropolitan centre'.[2] His upbringing in such an ambiguous land, when added to his innate personality traits, helps to explain the development of Wellington's personality.

The Wellesley family were a powerful part of the United Kingdom aristocracy that emerged after the Anglo-Scottish Union of 1707, but being Irish, rather than English or Scots, the family were something of outsiders. Wellington's elder brother Richard was created a marquess in the Irish rather than the socially superior British peerage in 1799. Richard was furious at this 'double gilt Potato', informing the Prime Minster of his 'bitter disappointment … at the ostensible mark of favour' bestowed by the King.[3] More positively, Wellington's experience in Ireland helped give him a rather more tolerant view of Roman Catholics than many of his English peers. In 1793 Arthur spoke in the Irish House of Commons in favour of a liberal policy towards Catholicism – this a major exception to his instinctive conservatism. The result of these influences was a withdrawn man who, in making his way in the army, a UK-wide institution that played a major role in forging the British identity, not least in the wars of the eighteenth and early nineteenth century, revealingly wrote that 'I like to walk alone'.[4]

Arthur Wesley (as the surname was spelled at the time) was probably born on 1 May 1769, in Dublin, although both date and place are uncertain. His mother, Anne, was the wife of Garret Wesley, Earl of Mornington and Professor of Music at Trinity College Dublin. Conceivably, Wellington's ancestors had arrived in Ireland some 600 years before his birth. His childhood was spent at the family seat of Dangan and in Dublin, before the family decamped to London. Some individuals show signs of great promise at a very young age. Arthur Wesley was not among their number. He was sent to Eton in 1781. There is no contemporary evidence that Wellington ever said that 'The Battle of Waterloo was won on the playing fields of Eton'. Far from being an enthusiast for team games, Arthur was a lonely, rather solitary boy. His father died in 1781, with the result that money became even tighter in a family that was by the standards of their peers already impecunious. Arthur was withdrawn from Eton in 1784 and went to live with his mother in Brussels (then a much cheaper place to live than London). Unlike Arthur, his brother Richard, the bright and ambitious new Earl of Mornington, was clearly going places.

Arthur was sent to France in 1786, to finish what passed for his education at the Royal Equitation Academy at Angers. In despair, his mother had declared him fit only as 'food for [gun] powder, and nothing more', and Richard had begun to pull strings to get his brother a career in the army. Although at Angers Arthur suffered from ill health, spending some enjoyable but scarcely profitable time on a sofa, playing with his pet terrier, this period marked a modest stepping-stone on the path to maturity. On catching sight of her son, Lady Mornington was struck by how he had physically grown up. The change was not just physical. The director of the Academy singled out 'one Irish lad of great promise, of the name of Wesley' one of the first times anyone caught a glimpse of the man Arthur was to come.[5] Alongside the practical skills he learned – familiarity with the French language, horse- and swordsmanship – Wesley grew in social confidence, and cemented his firm attachment to the world of the *ancien régime*. Within a few short years, this world was to collapse. That reactionary conservatism was to become one of the mainsprings of Wellington's character can surely be in large part traced back to Angers. While he was there, the French monarchy was approaching the crisis that was eventually to plunge the whole of Europe into turmoil. The storming of the Bastille occurred only two and a half years after Wesley left the Academy. Wesley's fate was to be closely bound up with fighting successive French regimes that destroyed the elegant world that he so admired.

Richard was seemingly less impressed by his younger brother's transformation. Writing to the Lord Lieutenant, he described Arthur as 'perfectly idle', but this letter was to end this idleness, for it was an appeal for a commission in the army for his sibling.[6] Arthur seems to have had no burning desire for a military career, and he was far from the only well-connected youth in the officer corps with this attitude. The army was in the doldrums in the 1780s. It was in the shadow of the American War of Independence, which had ended in 1783 with defeat, despite a generally creditable record. Swingeing cuts had reduced the army's numbers. While there were opportunities for active service overseas, in the reaches of the empire, for units stationed in Britain and Ireland the standard fare was internal security – all the more important in the absence of a police force. The army recruited from opposite ends of society, the officers being drawn from the social elite, and the rank and file from the poor. The gulf between the ranks was enormous, although shared experience on campaign and loyalty to regiment could build bridges.

On joining the army Arthur Wesley played the system for all it was worth – or perhaps he had the system played for him. Becoming an ensign in the 73rd Highlanders in 1787, he took advantage of his ability to 'purchase' commissions to move from regiment to regiment, gaining steps in rank as he did so. Purchase allowed rich but mediocre or even incompetent men to progress rapidly, with this huge disadvantage being occasionally balanced by the fact it allowed able officers with funds to get on in an army otherwise dominated by seniority. By April 1793, Wesley had held commissions in no less than seven regiments, but seems to have served with none of them except in the most perfunctory fashion. Wesley's time was spent in and around Dublin, where he served as an *aide-de-camp* to the Lord Lieutenant, and he became active in politics. In April 1790 he was elected to the Irish Parliament for the Wesley family seat of Trim. From this point onwards Wesley's career was to consist of politics intertwined with military affairs.

Gradually, however, Wesley began to take his military career more seriously. In 1793, he asked Lord Longford for permission to marry Longford's sister Catherine ('Kitty'). Arthur suffered the humiliation of being refused. In truth, he wasn't much of a catch. Stung, Wesley turned to his career, burning (or possibly giving away) his violin, dramatically making a break with his old self. Similarly, he paid less attention to the heavy gambling that was part of the life of the fashionable young man in Dublin, and concentrated on the minutiae of life as a regimental officer. Such a focused, painstaking, almost micromanaging approach was to characterise Wesley's subsequent career.

The events in France that eventfully led to the overthrow of the Bourbon monarchy had been initially greeted with enthusiasm across the Channel. As the situation became radicalised, conservative-minded people in Britain turned against the unfolding revolution. One man who became appalled by the events in France was Arthur Wesley. He spoke in the Irish House of Commons in January 1793, attacking the incarceration of King Louis XVI and the incursion of French troops into the Low Countries – the factor that eventually brought about war between Britain and France.

Wesley sought active service overseas, evidence of his newly discovered commitment to soldiering; this would also have had the advantage of removing him from the scene of his recent misfortunes. He accompanied his regiment, the 33rd Foot, when in June 1794 it was sent as part of a small British expedition to the Low Countries. Thanks to loans from Richard, Arthur had been able to buy a major's commission in the 33rd in April 1793, before purchasing a lieutenant colonelcy in the following September. So, thanks to the power of money, the 24-year-old Wesley, hitherto more of a courtier and politician than a real soldier, was first to see battle as the commander of an infantry battalion, with the lives of hundreds of men as his responsibility. Lieutenant Colonel Wesley had had no formal training for the role, and his first campaign was to be a brutal introduction to the realities of warfare.

3

Flanders and India, 1793–1804

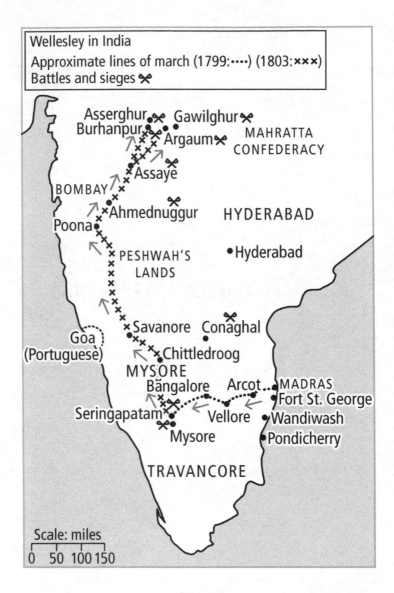

Wellesley in India
Approximate lines of march (1799:····) (1803:×××)
Battles and sieges ✖

Asserghur ✖ Gawilghur ✖
Burhanpur ✖
Argaum ✖   MAHRATTA
                  CONFEDERACY
✖ Assaye

BOMBAY
× Ahmednuggur ✖   HYDERABAD

Poona ●
×   ● Hyderabad
× PESHWAH'S
  LANDS

× Savanore   Conaghal ✖
Goa   ×
(Portuguese) × Chittledroog

MYSORE
Bangalore   Arcot ··· MADRAS
×   Fort St. George
Seringapatam × Vellore ● Wandiwash
✖   ● Pondicherry
Mysore

TRAVANCORE

Scale: miles
0 50 100 150

When war broke out between Britain and Revolutionary France in 1793 a British force commanded by King George III's son, the Duke of York, was deployed to Flanders, to cooperate with a smaller Dutch force and a much larger Austrian army. But the operations in this north-western corner of Europe were just one part of a much bigger picture. Not for the first time, or, as Wellington was to later experience, the last, coalition partners had very different strategic objectives. Following setbacks on the battlefield, in the summer of 1794 Austria decided to cut its losses in Flanders and concentrate on Germany and eastern Europe, abandoning its British ally. Fearing that ports of Nieuport and Ostend would fall into French hands, in June 1794 the British hastily deployed a force under Lord Moira to Flanders. Wesley's 33rd Foot sailed from Cork as part of this expedition.

This was a case of too little, too late. Moira was forced to retreat from Ostend, using the 33rd Foot as part of the rearguard brigade. (Some historians mistakenly place Wesley in command of the brigade). On 15 September 1794 Wesley had his first taste of combat, in a minor action at Boxtel. His battalion was covering the retirement of other units after a failed attack, when the 1st Guards was disordered by a retreating British cavalry unit. But as a

Guards officer recorded, the 33rd was 'formed in the rear, and opening to allow them to pass, wheeled up, and initially throwing a few cool and well-directed volleys into the enemy's squadrons obliged him to decamp precipitately' and the force was able to fall back unhindered.[7] While too much should not be made of a very minor clash conducted by an obscure officer, Colonel Wesley's calm leadership was certainly noticed by his superiors.

The retreating British eventually took up an apparently strong position on the River Waal, and the French closed up to the far side of the river. It was an active sector. Writing just before Christmas 1794 Wesley recorded that for six weeks the 33rd was near Nijmegan, holding the outposts:

> At present the French keep us in a perpetual state of alarm, we turn out once, sometimes twice, every night; the officers and men are harassed to death ... I have not had my clothes off my back for a long time, and generally spend the greatest part of the night upon the banks of the river.[8]

In early January 1795 the British retreated to the Rhine, and then, as the French continued their offensive, to the Ems. Wesley continued to command the 33rd – again, the claims of some historians that he commanded a brigade during the retreat are wishful thinking – until he went home on leave in early March. Famously, he was to say of his first campaign that, 'I learnt what one ought not to do, and that is always something'.[9]

Active service failed to set Arthur Wesley wholeheartedly onto the path of dedication to a military career. On his return from Germany he picked up his dormant political career, but failing to gain preferment, by the autumn of 1795 Wesley had resumed his military duties with the 33rd Foot. British strategy was increasingly focused on seizing enemy colonies, especially valuable sugar islands in the West Indies. The 33rd was sent to this theatre in November 1795, only for the convoy to be scattered by gales. The 33rd's ship limped back to England. The Duke of Wellington was given to talking about the 'finger of providence'; here is an early example of him having the course of his life changed by a factor quite beyond his control. Among British troops in the Caribbean in the 1790s, the mortality rate from sickness was appallingly high. Had the 33rd reached the West Indies, Arthur Wesley could all too easily have been among their number. Instead, the regiment was dispatched to India.

For an army officer to be sent to India in the late eighteenth century was a very different proposition to being sent to the Caribbean. While an early grave was always a distinct possibility, by taking exercise, and eating and drinking abstemiously (at least by the standards of contemporary British in India), Wesley kept his strength and built up his stamina to parallel his remarkable mental resilience. India offered the opportunity to make a reputation and a fortune. Frequent campaigning offered the chance for soldiers to build a career, and there was the example of Robert Clive, who in the mid eighteenth century amassed vast personal wealth in the process of carving out an empire. Many other soldiers and administrators had made smaller, but still substantial, fortunes. The British East India Company, supported by the government in London, through trade and conquest had made itself one of a number of significant powers on the subcontinent with the three 'presidencies' of Madras, Calcutta and Bombay. French power had been greatly reduced, but the British feared French influence in native states, especially the big three of south India: the Mahratta Confederacy, Hyderabad and Mysore. In the late 1790s there was an uneasy balance of power in the region, and it would have been by no means obvious to a contemporary observer that over the next half-century Britain would come to rule all India.

After recent disappointments, India offered Arthur Wesley a fresh chance. The formidable course of reading he set for himself on the long voyage out suggests that he was going to take it seriously. Wesley arrived at Calcutta in February 1797, and in the following summer more active service beckoned. An expedition was fitted out and sent against the colonies of France's allies, Spain and Holland, in the East Indies. The expedition, including Wesley and his 33rd Foot, got as far as Malaya before it was recalled to India. In mid 1797 he was but one lieutenant colonel among many; the fact that he had applied to command the force, but had been rebuffed, says much about his status. On Wesley's return to India, his fortunes were transformed, because Lord Mornington, his brother Richard, was appointed Governor General of India in October 1797. On hearing of his brother's elevation he had pessimistically written that given the 'rules respecting the disposal of all patronage in this country ... I can't expect to derive any advantage from it'.[10] While this might have been disingenuous, Mornington had thus far shown little respect for Arthur's views, or indeed anything else about him. However, Richard rapidly promoted Arthur into the circle of the Governor General's closest advisers. Another brother, Henry, had come out to India as the Governor General's private secretary.

The three Wellesleys (Richard had reverted to an earlier version of the name, and from May 1798 Arthur too used this spelling) were to have a huge impact on the position of the British in India. Like his younger brother, Mornington saw India as a golden opportunity to advance his career (and British interests: as far as he was concerned, they went hand in hand). This would be achieved, he soon decided, by a policy that was more aggressive than that of his predecessor. In the absence of rapid communications with London, and therefore supervision from home, by necessity Mornington had an extremely free hand in making and executing policy. As early as June 1798 there was an indication of both of this forward policy and Arthur's new role when Mornington asked his brother to prepare a memorandum on the possibility of war with Mysore. The East India Company had already fought three wars against this state. Now Tipoo Sultan, the ruler of Mysore, was flirting with France, employing French military advisers and even making a treaty with Paris. A successful campaign against Tipoo could thus strike a blow against two enemies.

Although Wellesley was now a man of influence, he was not the senior British military commander. Joining the staff of Lieutenant General George Harris, he proved his competence with his input into the logistic arrangements for the Mysore campaign. These were far from flawless, but Wellesley was to learn some valuable lessons for the future. This role perhaps went some way to overcoming the natural suspicion that he owed his appointment purely to his family connections (Wellesley was well aware that some officers believed that he was 'very little better than a spy').[11] Harris grew to appreciate Wellesley's qualities, and appointed him as adviser (de facto commander) to a force sent by a British ally, the Nizam of Hyderabad, which included British Indian (sepoy) battalions, and Wellesley's 33rd Foot. The nominal commander of the contingent, the Nizam's senior minister, Mir Allum, had requested Wellesley: the advantages of securing the services of the Governor General's brother were perfectly obvious. This appointment, which made sense politically and gave an opportunity to an officer who was increasingly demonstrating his competence, nevertheless caused jealousy, not least with Major General David Baird. He was an irascible Scot with a point to prove. Taken prisoner in a previous war, Baird had been chained in one of Tipoo's dungeons.

Alongside a mass of irregular infantry, Indian states deployed regular troops, drilled and trained by European mercenaries, who were perfectly capable of standing their ground and fighting in a European fashion. Other troops, such as 'pindaris', light cavalry that earned Wellesley's admiration, posed a threat to the supply lines of advancing British armies. In short, Wellesley's opponents were no pushovers, and there was nothing predetermined about the British victories.

The campaign began in early March 1799, and on the 27th there was a substantial clash between the armies at Malavelly. Wellesley's 33rd Foot played a subsidiary but useful role in the defeat of the Mysorean army. However, Wellesley's career nearly came to inglorious and premature end on the night of 5/6 April 1799. As the army approached Tipoo's capital of Seringapatam, as a preliminary to the siege, General Harris ordered Wellesley to clear Sultanpettah Topi , an area of coconut and palm groves. The attack was mounted at night without Wellesley having had the opportunity to properly reconnoitre the ground. Although the 33rd overcame the surprise of finding the feature occupied by Mysorean infantry, Wellesley lost control of his men among the pitch-dark trees and undergrowth. The attack was a complete failure. Wellesley personally reported the failure to Harris and, if reports are to be believed, later noisily gave way to self-pity, wailing that his career was wrecked. Such stories are almost certainly exaggerated slurs put about by envious rivals, but there is no reason to doubt that the affair dented Wellesley's *amour propre*, if only in the short term. In military terms it was an inconsequential action, and on 26 April Wellesley redeemed his reputation with a successful attack on some of Seringapatam's outlying defences.

The assault on the city on 4 May was entrusted to Baird, and it was rapidly captured. Tipoo Sultan was killed.

Wellesley was appointed to command the captured city – an appointment that once again outraged Baird. Wellesley ruthlessly ended the sacking of the city, hanging and flogging. Over the next three years he showed that he was a highly effective administrator, with vast responsibility and a great deal of freedom of action. Wellesley's Mysore years were crucial in honing his administrative and political skills. Similarly, in mid 1800, Wellesley commenced his first operation as an independent commander, a campaign that served to complete his apprenticeship in the military sphere.

Wellesley's opponent was Dhoondiah Wao, a warlord who had gathered a substantial military force, taking advantage of the confusion in Mysore to build a power base. Dhoondiah posed a distinct threat to the security of Mysore and, ultimately, British India. Wellesley's campaign saw him develop an effective political/military counterinsurgency strategy (to use a modern term). Leading a small army to hunt down Dhoondiah, Wellesley placed emphasis on gaining intelligence to find his elusive enemy and operated a strategy of clearing areas of enemy troops and then securing them with garrisons and forts. In Wellesley's words, this brought about the 'greatest of all blessings for Troops, a quiet rear [area], and a secure communication with our own country'.[12] By offering a large reward for Dhoondiah, Wellesley hoped to destabilise him. Relentlessly pursued, his stronghold captured, and deprived of food, Dhoondiah's army began to melt away. On 10 September 1800 Wellesley at last caught up with Dhoondiah at Conaghal and smashed his army. Dhoondiah was killed. This campaign was an extremely significant point in Arthur Wellesley's learning process. Drawing upon his experience in the Seringapatam campaign, Wellesley carried out what he described as 'light and quick movements', that were reliant on mobility and aggressive action, and the results validated his approach. As a by-product he gained more experience of coalition warfare. His Indian allies were essential in providing support, especially in guarding his lines of communication. All these lessons were to be of great value in future campaigns. After this campaign, no one could seriously doubt that Wellesley was much more than simply the Governor General's brother.

Wellesley was promoted to major general in April 1802. His career had suffered an apparent setback in 1801 when he hoped to command an expedition, only to be superseded by Baird. The supersession led to frosty relations with Richard, now Marquess Wellesley, who had failed to support him. Nonetheless, Richard gave Arthur a leading role in dealings with the Marathas, which were moving towards crisis point. The Confederation was engulfed in civil war. Lord Wellesley used the turmoil to improve the British position, with his brother rather more sceptical about the need for war. The first rumblings of the avalanche came in 1800 when one of the five major Maratha rulers, Jeswant Rao Holkar, defeated two rivals. In May 1803 General Wellesley led a bloodless expedition to Poona, to put the Peshwa, now a British client, back on his throne. A delicate diplomatic gavotte followed, with Arthur Wellesley at the centre but as the executor of policy rather than its author. In the long term, there is no doubt that Lord Wellesley was determined to reduce Maratha independence and power, but in mid 1803 the armies of Scindia and the Rajah of Berar threatened Hyderabadi territory. Lord Wellesley had General Wellesley deliver an ultimatum to the Maratha chiefs, which led to war.

The British invasion force consisted of two columns, one under Arthur Wellesley, and the other under Colonel James Stevenson (far away to the north was another army under General Lake). On 8 August 1803 Wellesley seized the initiative when he struck at Ahmednuggar. In keeping with his 'light and quick' concept, the walled town was taken by escalade, an immediate assault using storming ladders, rather than waiting for the walls to be breached by artillery in a formal siege. The fort fell on the 12th. Thereafter the campaign did not go so smoothly. Lacking the intelligence that had proved so vital in his last campaign, the Marathas proved an elusive enemy, and it was not until 23 September that Wellesley met the enemy army in open battle. He did so at a numerical disadvantage. Stevenson's column had yet to arrive, and the disparity in numbers concerned him. But Wellesley feared that if he delayed the Marathas might slip away, and the wearisome pursuit would have to begin all over again. His army of British and sepoy units was just 7,000 strong, with 5,000 Indian irregular cavalry. The Marathas had perhaps 50,000 men, the core of which was 10,000 European-trained infantry and powerful artillery.

The resulting battle, Assaye, was, Wellesley believed, 'the bloodiest for the numbers that I ever saw'.[13] He prevailed through his boldness in attacking, which bordered on recklessness, and by extremely hard fighting by the sepoys and British infantry and cavalry. Wellesley led from the front and was in constant danger. His horse, Diomed, was skewered by a pike. Wellesley had underestimated his enemy: this not a light, irregular force such as Dhoondiah's. The enemy infantry was 'the best I have seen in India excepting our own ... I assure you that their fire was so heavy that I much doubted at one time whether I should be able to prevail upon our troops to advance'.[14] And yet, British and Indian alike, Wellesley's men had advanced and won a victory which he came to rate above those he fought in the Peninsula, and even Waterloo.

More fighting remained to be done. At Arguam (29 November) Wellesley, now united with Stevenson's force, crushed another Maratha army The culmination of Wellesley's campaign was the storming and capture of the fortress of Gawilghur in December. In the face of these blows, and Lake's no less remarkable victories in the north, Scindia and the Rajah of Berar ended the war on British terms. Arthur Wellesley's campaigning days in India were over. Although a fresh war broke out with Holkar in 1804, he did not get actively involved. Sick, aware that Lord Wellesley was to be replaced as Governor General, and tiring of India, he decided it was time to return home.

India was Arthur Wellesley's apprenticeship as a high commander. In his years there he developed an inherently aggressive style of warfare, seeking to seize the initiative, impose his will on the enemy and keep them off balance. He also gained invaluable experience of coalition warfare, in handling delicate relations with Indian allies, and in the political aspects of command, no less demanding because his political superior was his own brother. In short, his successes in India demonstrated that Wellesley possessed military genius.

4

General in waiting, 1805–1808

On returning to Britain, Wellesley had a modest reputation founded on his Indian exploits. This certainly put him in the frame for a future command, but prejudice against 'sepoy generals' and the dislike of the commander-in chief, the King's brother the Duke of York, seemed to limit his chances of advancement. An alternative career in politics looked more promising. Wellesley was consulted by the Prime Minister, William Pitt the Younger, who was impressed. Moreover, Wellesley renewed his friendship with Robert Stewart, Lord Castlereagh, whom he had known in Dublin in the 1790s. Castlereagh was Secretary of State for War and the Colonies, and was to prove a formidable ally in the months and years ahead.

When waiting for a meeting with Castlereagh in September 1805, Wellesley met Vice Admiral Lord Nelson, Britain's greatest naval commander. Initially, Nelson showed off horribly, until he left the room, discovered the major general's identity, and then resumed the discussion, but in a very different vein. If he had had only their initial conversation to go on, Wellesley would have judged Nelson as having 'a light and trivial character', but then the admiral 'talked like an officer and a statesman ... I don't know that I ever had a conversation that interested me more'.[15] This occasion was the only time that these two titans ever met. Within six weeks Nelson was to die at the Battle of Trafalgar. Nelson is usually portrayed as having no idea who the bronzed soldier was, but actually the two men had corresponded while Wellesley was in India. This suggests that Wellington's recollection of the meeting, which implies that the two men did not introduce themselves, is accurate – or that Nelson's memory failed him on this occasion.

Wellesley became a Westminster MP in April 1806, combining his parliamentary duties with military life, commanding a brigade on the Kent coast. This was a considerable comedown for the victor of Assaye, but it was at this time he made his famous statement of his conception of duty:

> I am nimmuckwallah … I have ate [*sic*] of the King's salt, and, therefore, I conceive it to be my duty to serve with unhesitating zeal and cheerfulness, when and wherever the King or his government may think proper to employ me. [16]

This can be read was the statement of an ambitious and politically well-connected officer biding his time, and he was noticeably keen to divest himself of his government post when he was appointed to an overseas command in 1807. However, Wellesley had acquired a highly developed sense of duty and responsibility. Had his career remained stuck at this modest level Wellesley's attitudes may have changed, but in the medium term a combination of duty and a sense that the army had more to offer meant he was prepared to wait.

A major change in Wellesley's life came with his marriage to Kitty Packenham in April 1806. Wellesley had not been celibate in India – there were rumours of liaisons with married women – but, amazingly, he had had no contact with Kitty, not even a letter, during his time in the East, and their first meeting in a decade took place at the wedding ceremony. Sadly, the marriage soon proved that it was not a love match, at least not on his side, and biographers have wrestled with his motives for marrying a women who was no longer young and losing her physical attraction. Validation of his achievements was probably part of it. Denied her hand as a penniless officer with no obvious career prospects, Wellesley now claimed her as a rich and successful general. Arthur and Kitty produced two sons but the partners were too dissimilar in personalities for the marriage to be a success. Wellesley's military career was characterised by careful planning followed by decisive action. In determining upon marriage with Kitty so soon after his return from India, he showed plenty of the latter quality but little of the former.

While his military career appeared to have plateaued, in April 1807 Wellesley became a member of the government as Chief Secretary for Ireland. The insurrection of 1798 was still a raw memory. In 1801 Britain and Ireland had been joined in an act of union, with the Irish parliament abolished. This move was undertaken largely for strategic reasons, and Wellesley soon discovered that it was not popular among the mass of the Irish people. He took a pessimistic view of the situation in Ireland, and recognised that the one thing that might lessen resentment – easing the anti-Catholic law – had been ruled out by George III's adamant opposition. Wellesley (and his brother Richard on his behalf) lobbied for an active military command. Wellesley was consulted over a possible expedition to South America, and when in June 1807 he was offered a brigade in an expedition to Denmark, it came as welcome relief from the mire of Irish politics. Wellesley in effect took a sabbatical from his government job.

In 1807 the neutral Danes were the victim of Britain's ruthless determination to ensure its security. Napoleon's 'Continental System' aimed to wreck the British economy by preventing trade with Europe, and as a consequence he cast his eyes on the Baltic coast. The Danish fleet would also be a useful addition to Napoleon's naval strength, depleted by Trafalgar. The British move was intended to forestall such an outcome. The expedition arrived off Denmark in August 1807. Diplomacy having failed, Wellesley's brigade was the first part of the British army to land on Danish soil. On 29 August he scattered a Danish force advancing towards Copenhagen in an action at Kioge, and, following the bombardment of the Danish capital, Wellesley, with two other officers, was sent to negotiate the Danish surrender. He was conciliatory, recognising that by making off with the Danish fleet and naval stores in return for the withdrawal of British troops, the object of the expedition had been obtained and it was pointless to insist on harsher terms.

The Copenhagen expedition proved an important milestone in Arthur Wellesley's career. He once again proved his competence as a commander – this time in Europe, not far away in India, and his reputation in the army grew. The military and political skills that he demonstrated in this campaign greatly enhanced his prospects of securing a major command in future. That opportunity arose within twelve months of the Baltic campaign. Attempting to enforce the Continental System, in his megalomania Napoleon turned on his ally, Spain. In May 1808 this provoked an insurrection, exacerbated when Napoleon seated his brother, Joseph, on the Spanish throne. The door had been flung wide open for Britain to take advantage. Wellesley was appointed to command an expedition to Portugal, where intelligence suggested that the inhabitants had risen against General Junot's small French army of occupation.

Wellesley came ashore on 1 August 1808 and on the 17th defeated a small French force at Roliça. Overshadowed by later, much larger battles, Roliça is notable both as Wellesley's first victory over the French and for being an aggressive, offensive operation, indicating that he believed the methods used in India were also suitable for use against Napoleon's army. After winning a defensive victory at Vimeiro (21 August) he was superseded by two officers, Generals Burrard and Dalrymple; Wellesley's entreaties to capitalise on the victory were ignored and instead negotiations began with Junot. By the Convention of Cintra, the French agreed to evacuate Portugal, but they were to be conveyed in British ships, and permitted to carry their loot (taken from Britain's Portuguese ally) with them. Wellesley made his clear his opposition, but in the end signed the document. If he signed it, he risked political unpopularity. If he withheld his signature, he could have been accused of petulance and disloyalty to his superiors. Neither were attractive options, but Wellesley probably chose the greater evil, and in doing so imperilled his military career. Disillusioned, he returned to Britain in early October.

When news of Cintra was made public there was uproar. Dalrymple, Burrard and Wellesley were pilloried in the press. An inquiry cleared all three men, but the affair finished the active military careers of the two senior officers. Wellesley survived, in part because something like the true story emerged in the course of the proceedings. Generals with a proven record of victory were few and far between in the British army of 1808, and were not lightly discarded.

5

From Oporto to Talavera, 1809

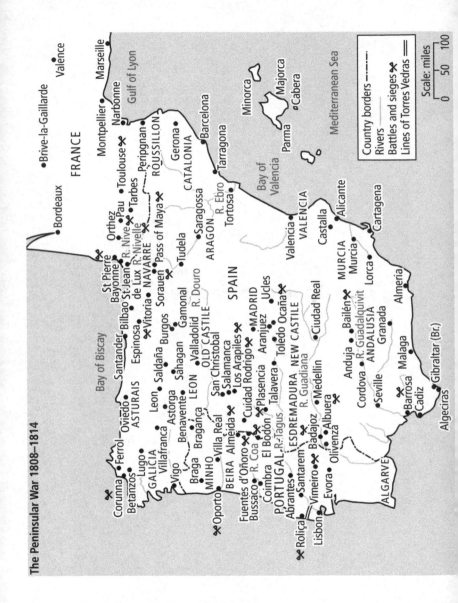

The Peninsular War 1808–1814

Cleared by the Board of Inquiry, Wellesley waited to see if would be given the chance to return to the Peninsula. In his absence, Sir John Moore had taken command in Portugal and had led his small army into Spain on a campaign that would go down as one of the epics of British military history. At Corunna, on 16 January 1809, Moore's army was victorious and was evacuated safely by the Royal Navy, but its commander was killed. The campaign helped relieve the pressure on Spanish armies at a crucial stage, and from Wellesley's selfish point of view, his main rival for command – and the only one of his contemporaries who had demonstrated anything like the same level of competence as a general – had been removed from the equation.

Wellesley, looking on from England, applied his mind to the situation in the Iberian Peninsula, and in March 1809 wrote a memorandum for the government. Wellesley stated 'that Portugal might be defended, whatever might be the result of the contest in Spain'. He recognised that given Britain's dominance at sea, which would enable an unending stream of supplies to be dispatched by ship, Portugal could be held by a small army of 20,000 supported by Portuguese forces suitably reorganised by the British (undoubtedly, Wellesley had the model of

British-officered Indian sepoy units in mind). Portugal could then be used as a base for operations into Spain, which he believed, could not be conquered by the French. In short, the war in Spain and Portugal offered the British, for the first time since the 1790s, the opportunity to conduct a major campaign on the continent of Europe.[17]

A month after submitting his appreciation, Wellesley received the news for which he had longed: he was to return to Portugal as commander. This time he burned his bridges, resigning his government post and parliamentary seat. Wellesley's activities in Portugal in 1809 offer further testimony to his military genius. He reorganised the army, forming it into 'divisions' that enhanced cohesion by creating permanent higher formations. Wellesley placed William Beresford in command of the Portuguese army with a mandate to reform it. It was an inspired appointment; Beresford's reform of the Portuguese forces was hugely successful. Alongside the British and Portuguese troops served the King's German Legion, an exile army of excellent quality that had its origins in the old Hanoverian army. By the end of the Peninsular War, the Anglo-German-Portuguese army had become a formidably effective force. Its success was founded on excellent raw material; Wellesley's reorganisation; operational experience that included the learning and application of hard-won lessons; and, of course, a supremely competent commander.

Based at Lisbon, Wellesley's position was potentially threatened by Soult's French forces at Oporto, Portugal's second city, and two other French armies, under Marshals

Victor and Ney respectively, in separate locations across the Spanish border. If the various French forces united they could overwhelm the British by sheer numbers, but geographically separated as they were, they invited defeat in detail. Wellesley seized the initiative by moving against Soult. Arriving at the River Douro on 12 May, he looked across at Oporto, held by the French, who had destroyed the only bridge in the area and removed all boats – or so they thought. Actually, the locals revealed the whereabouts of concealed wine barges, which Wellesley used to ferry British troops across the river to a large, and undefended, seminary. By the time Soult woke up to the situation, the British were in the city in force, and he was compelled to retreat. Worse, because British forces had also crossed the Douro elsewhere and blocked off possible retreat routes, Soult was forced to abandon his baggage. Wellesley had won a stunning victory which freed Portugal at a small cost to his army.

Late in life, the Duke of Wellington compared French commanders' methods in the Peninsula with his own:

> They planned their campaigns just as you might make a splendid piece of harness. It looks very well; and answers very well; until it gets broken; and then you are done for. Now I made my campaigns of ropes. If anything went wrong, I tied a knot; and went on.[18]

In other words, in contrast to the French marshals (no push-overs as opponents) Wellington had a flexible and pragmatic approach. He had previously shown this mental agility in India, but at Oporto Wellesley demonstrated the maturity of his talent as an extraordinarily accomplished general. Given the opportunity to get troops across the river, Wellesley seized it with both hands, and launched an audacious attack, which reaped rich rewards.

The victory at Oporto opened up an array of strategic possibilities. Receiving assurances from the local Spanish junta that they would supply his army, after a halt to regroup, Wellesley determined to advance into Spain, towards Talavera, to attack Victor's army. He would be cooperating with a Spanish force under the elderly General Cuesta. Coalition operations always add a layer of complexity, and Wellesley was to find his Spanish counterpart a particularly testing partner. After crossing into Spain the British commander rapidly discovered that the promises of logistic support he had received were worthless, and his army began to run alarmingly short of supplies.

Cuesta has become one of the pantomime villains of British military history. While he was undoubtedly an appallingly bad general, Cuesta had reason to resent the much younger man, who he feared would supplant him. They had no common language; Wellesley turned up late for a meeting because his guide became lost; and in general there was an absence of empathy and trust between the two men. Eventually, the commanders agreed to attack Victor early in the morning of 23 July. At the appointed hour, the Spanish army was noticeably absent. In a farcical scene, Wellesley eventually discovered Cuesta asleep, and the old general compounded his crime by casually telling his ally that Spanish army was too tired to fight that day. Perhaps to demonstrate his independence, Cuesta on 24 July rashly advanced without British support. He was promptly defeated and forced back. The consequence was that the British and Spanish armies found themselves being attacked at Talavera on 27 July by Victor's forces, which had been reinforced by the army of King Joseph.

At Talavera the British, holding low hills, bore the brunt of the French attacks, which came dangerously close to succeeding. Nonetheless Wellesley's calm generalship saw his army through to a resounding victory, albeit with heavy loses. Wellesley was all too aware that he had achieved a mere tactical success. He could not follow up his victory and was short of the supplies that the Spanish had failed to provide. Unwilling to cooperate with Cuesta a moment longer than necessary, and with his supply-lines threatened by a French force from the north, on 3 August Wellesley retired to the Portuguese border. The march was a difficult one, which placed the discipline of the army under severe strain, with Wellesley railing in a general order against looting. Wellesley's otherwise calm demeanour in the face of tremendous pressures was a huge asset during the retreat. For reasons of coalition diplomacy Wellesley was careful not to cross immediately back into Portugal, but he fully realised that any major co-operation with Spanish armies was, for the foreseeable future, futile. Instead, he concentrated on the defence of Portugal.

In October, Wellesley, with his engineers, reconnoitred the area north of Lisbon, and decided to build defensive positions, to which the army could retreat in times of need. Wellesley knew that Napoleon was once again victorious against Austria, and the Emperor might well next lead a large army into Spain. The 'Lines of Torres Vedras', built over the next few months, consisted of two defensive systems of over 150 forts and strongpoints with 534 guns, largely garrisoned by Portuguese militia. A third, much shorter, line covered a position where, if necessary, troops could be embarked on ships and Portugal abandoned altogether, although Wellesley remained confident that the country could be held. A British engineer engaged on the Lines hailed the scheme as demonstrating 'the foresight and skill of the general and the exertion of the engineer … in happy unison'.[19] He was correct. The Lines of Torres Vedras showed yet again that Arthur Wellesley possessed considerable strategic imagination.

As commander of the army in the Peninsula Wellesley had to write a good many routine letters. One, penned on 16 September 1809 to the British ambassador in Lisbon, had an uncharacteristically self-conscious addendum: 'This is the first time I have signed my new name'.[20] In August he had been created Viscount Wellington of Talavera and Wellington. The name was chosen by his brother William, there being no time to consult Arthur, far away in Portugal, and he had alighted upon the Somerset town of Wellington, near the village of Welleslie. Over the next six years the new peer was to make the name of Wellington famous across the globe.

6

'The cautious system', 1810

Wellington's experience of attempting to cooperate with Cuesta at Talavera had left deep scars. On a visit to Cadiz he sought to persuade the Spanish Supreme Junta to keep their armies on the defensive and train their soldiers. Wellington had no illusions that 'these people' would heed his sound advice: 'they will persist in fighting great battles... and one after another their armies will be destroyed'.[21] A Spanish army had won a famous victory over the French at Bailén in 1808, which helped to convince the Spanish they were capable of victory without British support. But at Ocaña, in November 1809, a Spanish army suffered one of the most shattering defeats of the entire Peninsular War. Wellington, who had politely but firmly refused requests to take the offensive alongside the Spaniards, now prepared for a third French invasion of Portugal.

Wellington assessed that the main blow would come via the fortress cities of Ciudad Rodrigo and Almeida, and so he stationed the bulk of his army there under his personal command, with detachments covering other possible invasion routes. Wellington deployed the Light Division under the command of Brigadier General Robert Craufurd in front of the main army, where the British and Portuguese light infantry and riflemen were highly effective in screening Wellington's main force: the French advanced virtually blindly. Wellington's intuition was correct, and he found himself up against a formidable opponent. Although Napoleon chose to remain in Paris, the invasion forces was commanded by Marshal André Masséna. When the two men met after the war, Wellington told Masséna that he had given him some nasty moments, while the Marshal replied that Wellington had turned his hair grey. [22] The situation for the Anglo-Portuguese army could have been worse. The French had five corps in Spain, but the need to hold areas infested by guerrillas, and to watch against Spanish armies (which despite constant defeats always seemed to bounce back) meant that not all could be sent against Wellington. There was no effective commander-in-chief in theatre, and given the extreme rivalries among the French commanders, co-operation was sorely lacking.

While preparing to fight Masséna, Wellington also faced the problem of shoring up political support at home. The government fell in October 1809. The new Prime Minister, Spencer Perceval, appointed Richard Wellesley as foreign secretary, and Lord Liverpool, an ally of Wellington, went to the War Office. Yet Wellington's position was by no means secure. The retreat after Talavera had caused a backlash in England, and many in the country, and some members of the government, feared that the campaign in the Peninsula was ultimately doomed. Wellington's constant demands for funds for his army (he feared being 'destroyed for want of money'[23]) also went down badly with the Cabinet. Perhaps the greatest problem is that Wellington believed (not without reason) that he dare not share his plans with his political masters for fear that they would leak and appear in the press. The most he could do was prepare them in general terms for another campaign that 'would necessarily be defensive'. In the short term, this would appear disappointing: 'there may be no brilliant events'. Wellington's concern for security put his relationship with Liverpool, who had to defend him in parliament, under some strain. It is to the credit of both men that the general accepted responsibility for the consequences, and the politicians (and indeed the government) allowed Wellington the 'exercise of my own judgement'.[24] Wellington had staked his career, reputation and, conceivably, his very life on his strategy being successful.

In June 1810 Masséna besieged the key Spanish frontier fortress of Cuidad Rodrigo, which fell on 10 July. Wellington came under pressure to attack the French. Even some in his own army were critical, but Wellington was looking well beyond short-term measures to a strategy that would bring ultimate success. His ability to divine the correct strategic path, and the self-confidence and moral courage to not to be diverted from it by personal unpopularity and political pressures, were crucial to Wellington's greatness as a general.

With one fortress captured, Masséna advanced on Almeida, Cuidad Rodrigo's Portuguese twin. Marshal Ney's French forces on 24 July 1810 fought a sharp action with the Light Division, a drawn battle that nonetheless drove Craufurd's men across the River Coa. Wellington had 'positively forbidden' such 'foolish affairs', but viewed Crauford's mistake as 'one of judgement, not of intention'.[25] While Wellington was quite capable of giving an errant subordinate a withering rebuke, he did not do so on this occasion. He prized 'Black Bob' too highly, and there was no need: Craufurd became aware of Wellington's displeasure, and was mortified by it. Thus did Wellington handle a valued subordinate.

On 15 August, it was Almeida's turn to be besieged by the French. A freak cannon shell blew up the magazine, and Almeida surrendered on 28 August. This was a potentially devastating blow to Wellington's campaign, as the French army captured supplies and had gained a base from which it could operate, but he simply 'tied a knot' and carried on. The ability to respond to problems of 'friction' is the mark of a great commander. Not for the first or the last time, Wellington demonstrated that very quality. Wellington fell back and his army took up position on Bussaco ridge, a dominating feature that blocked Masséna's route of advance. On 27 September 1810 the French launched a series of attacks, which the Anglo-Portuguese army, skilfully deployed in defence, repulsed after stiff fighting. Wellington only ever saw this as being a delaying action, and so he recommended his retreat, getting safely inside the Lines of Torres Vedras by 10 October.

That the French knew nothing about the Lines before they arrived before them was a tribute to Wellington's obsession with security, but also was a considerable intelligence failure on the part of the French. Masséna was in an unenviable position: stuck in front of effectively impregnable defences, at the end of long supply lines harassed by Portuguese irregulars, in a country largely swept clear of food, thanks to Wellington's ruthless scorched-earth strategy. His opponent, on the other hand, was kept in supply by sea, so while the French army grew progressively weaker, Wellington's grew stronger. Attrition played strongly to his advantage.

Wellington's strategy brought a crop of political problems. The Portuguese population in the devastated territories beyond Lisbon suffered dreadfully. Wellington appealed for the British government's help, to no avail. On this and other issues Wellington was forced to cope with fierce critics inside the Portuguese government, and the Spaniards were less than impressed by his inactivity. At home, the initial euphoria over the news of Bussaco had evaporated when Wellington continued to retreat. Now, apparently passive behind the Lines of Torres Vedas, with the costs of the campaign ballooning, there was a renewed crisis in London. Wellington showed poor judgement by issuing demands for more men and money for his army (and writing scathing private letters bemoaning his lack of support), at a time when he was being urged to save money, and when a hard-pressed ministry was doing its best to aid him. Towards the end of 1810, King George III fell victim to 'madness' (most likely porphyria) and it seemed possible that the Prince Regent would put the opposition Whigs into government – and they might abandon the expensive and apparently never-ending war in the Peninsula. This fear formed the context for Wellington's decision making until in February 1811 'Prinny' confirmed the Perceval government in office.

Thus Wellington was under pressure to take the offensive. A successful attack might strengthen his position at home. But he realised that, by not losing, he was winning. So even before the inevitable French retreat began, Wellington had:

> … determined to persevere in my cautious system, to operate on the flanks and rear of the enemy with my small and light detachments, and thus force them out of Portugal by the distresses they will suffer, and do them all the mischief I can upon their retreat. [26]

Wellington held his nerve. In March 1811 Masséna finally retreated. Portugal was liberated and the country was never threatened again. Wellington's attritional 'cautious system' had prevailed. It was one of his greatest victories.

7

The Commander and His Army

Wellington had a rare combination of talents. At the highest levels of war, he was a brilliant strategist and war manager, but he was also an inspirational leader, to be found in the place of danger in battle. He excelled in all of these roles, and this is what set him aside from all but a handful of his contemporaries. His success was founded on hard work, a thorough grasp of detail, and a deep understanding of the complexity of his job: the interplay of strategy with the lower levels of war, and the critical role of factors such as politics, economics, intelligence and logistics. His style of warfare was inherently aggressive. Wellington sought to seize the initiative, impose his will on the enemy and keep them off balance. This was to court risks, but his judgement on how far those risks should be pushed was well developed. He learned from experience and had the rare 'fingertip feeling' that allowed him to 'read' a battle. His intuition was a product of study and experience. Late in life, Wellington declared that, 'All the business of war, and indeed all the business of life, is to endeavour to find out what you don't know by what you do; that's what I called "guessing what was at the other side of the hill".'[27]

Intelligence and logistics were never far from Wellington's thoughts. Having made good use of *hircarrahs* (spies) in India, when commanding a brigade in Denmark in 1807 he rued the absence of such sources of intelligence in a hostile population. The Iberian Peninsula was to prove more fertile ground. Guerrillas were a ready source of information, and he was well served by talented intelligence officers such as George Scovell and Colquhoun Grant. Intelligence was linked to logistics. If supplies were short, soldiers were prone to pillage and therefore alienate the local population, which could mean sources of intelligence drying up.

High command demands political and administrative as well as military skills. Wellington's record in handling complex relations with the British and Allied governments, and dealing with coalition commanders, was good but not unblemished. His petulant, whinging letters to ministers in London, which showed his unwillingness to appreciate their perspective, was one of his worst failings. The likes of Liverpool, Castlereagh and Bathurst showed great tolerance in putting up with such behaviour. Part of Wellington's success lay in taking an existing army that had nothing very much wrong with it – Moore's campaign in 1809 had shown that – and turning it into a highly effective instrument of war. He did this without changing its fundamental character as an *ancien régime* army, which contrasted starkly with its French opponents. Napoleon's army was a mass conscript force that offered genuine opportunities for poor but talented solders to rise to the top. It made use of thick skirmish lines and dense column formations, not least because troops lacked the training and rigid discipline essential to fight in line. Wellington's army was a small, long-service force of volunteers recruited from the lower reaches of society and officered by the upper classes, which relied on eighteenth-century linear tactical methods.

Wellington's characteristic methods had plenty of precedents. They included deploying his men, sometimes lying down, behind the crest of a ridgeline to protect them from enemy fire; using his men in a two-deep line (rather than three-deep, as per the tactical manual) to ensure that every infantryman could fire his musket; and putting out a screen of skirmishers in front of the battle line to counter the enemy's light troops. What Wellington did differently was to ensure that these methods worked better than ever before; for instance, by stiffening the skirmish line with companies of rifle-armed troops, and by successfully integrating Portuguese units into British formations. His use of artillery was conservative. He tended to parcel guns out along the line, rather than mass them in grand batteries in the French style. Wellington's use of cavalry also tended to be cautious, which reflected both the frequent weakness of his mounted force, and his bitter experience of its unreliability. Although one can exaggerate the ineffectiveness of British cavalry, there were occasions, from the 23rd Light Dragoons at Talavera to the Union Brigade at Waterloo, when British cavalry got wildly out of hand in the charge. Wellington denounced cavalry officers for 'galloping at every thing'.[28] While unfair as a generalisation, Wellington had been bitten once too often.

Wellington was not a charismatic leader in the Napoleonic mould. He was essentially a loner, with a forbidding personality, although he could be good company and inspired affection from his military 'family' (staff). His headquarters were simple, unpretentious, even austere, affairs, which reflected his personality (although after 1815 he had an expensive lifestyle). A junior staff officer recalled that depending on Wellington's mood (which was affected by news from home or the battlefront) dinner could be lively 'when the conversation was constant & general' – alternatively, 'scarce anyone dare open his mouth except to take in his dinner'.[29]

Wellington was about 5 feet 9 inches tall, and was handsome with piercing blue eyes. His most prominent feature was his aquiline nose, which gave him the nickname of 'Old Nosey' among the men. Although the Napoleonic Wars was an era of gaudy uniforms, on campaign Wellington preferred to dress plainly, in semi-civilian garb. In 1813 a junior officer 'was much struck with the simplicity' of [Wellington's] attire ... a very light grey pelisse coat – single-breasted, without a sash – and a white neck-handkerchief [and] a cocked hat'.[30]

One of Wellington's faults was his failure to give praise when it was due – something he seemingly came to regret later in life. His offhand dismissal of the role of the Royal Artillery in his Waterloo dispatch caused deep resentment. Wellington was also capable of withering sarcasm, or worse, towards individuals. Alexander Gordon, who saw long service on Wellington's staff, liked as well as admired his chief, but witnessed his less pleasant side. Once, Gordon wrote home that Wellington 'has no idea of gratitude, favour or affection, and cares not for anyone however much he may owe to him or find him useful'. This was unfair, and probably reflected Gordon's poor personal morale on that particular day. Ironically, Wellington's reaction to Gordon's death, after he was wounded at Waterloo, showed another dimension to his character. The Duke said 'in a voice tremulous with emotion, "Well, thank God! I don't know what it is to lose a battle, but certainly nothing can be more painful than to gain one with the loss of so many of one's friends".'[31] The mask of command, which Wellington had worn to enable him to cope with the enormous pressure of generalship, had slipped. Wellington was not heartless, but he had iron self-control.

Given his acerbic approach, it is scarcely surprising that Wellington did not have an equivalent of Admiral Lord Nelson's 'Band of Brothers'. Nelson's method of command was to set a broad plan but then rely on his ships' captains' initiative in executing it. This approach required the highest levels of mutual trust and understanding. Such 'mission command' was alien to Wellington. 'I am obliged to be everywhere, and if absent from any operation, something goes wrong,' he declared, and while this was unfair on competent generals such as Hill and Graham, it was not entirely without foundation.[32] He simply did not have that degree of trust in his subordinates. Before Waterloo Wellington refused to reveal his plans to Lord Uxbridge, his second-in-command and thus the man who would have to lead the army if the Duke was killed; and if his orders were disobeyed he was capable of fury. This was not a command culture that encouraged initiative.

In fairness, there was a big difference between the two services. Nelson's captains were experienced, talented professionals. By contrast, the army was an organisation that was far less professional, in both the literal and the 'expert' senses of the word. Wellington was saddled with some quite senior subordinates who were poor at their jobs. This seems to have reinforced his natural tendency to be a centraliser. He did not have a staff in the modern sense, and in his early Peninsular campaigns more or less acted as his own chief of staff. From 1810 onwards Wellington grew to rely on George Murray, his Quartermaster General, to do the detailed staff work, and even allowed him some leeway in using his initiative; but unlike the relationship of near equality between the Prussian commander Blücher and his chief of staff, Gneisenau, Murray was always the servant.

On the battlefield, Wellington was courageous. Wellington was nearly captured while out on a personal reconnaissance just before Talavera, and could have been killed or wounded numerous times on many battlefields. At Waterloo, Wellington rode into an infantry square just ahead of French cuirassiers. An officer commented that, 'Our Commander-in-Chief, as far as I could judge, appeared perfectly composed; but looked very thoughtful and pale'. Wellington's habitual calmness was an important facet of his leadership. By showing himself in the front line, with the mask of command obscuring whatever anxiety he might have felt, he offered reassurance to his soldiers. Corporal John Douglas recorded the army's 'most unbounded confidence in the skill, courage and coolness of Wellington ... [they] always considered themselves sure of victory when led by him', which led to 'an enthusiasm [to fight] not to be overcome'.[33] Wellington did not earn the love of the common soldier – he was too patrician, too austere for that; – but he earned their respect and trust. It was not just British rank and file who had this confidence in Wellington. In 1815 before the Waterloo campaign commenced, a Hanoverian officer recorded that Wellington's 'appearance inspired and confirmed our trust in his generalship which foretold victory'.[34]

Famously, Wellington referred to his troops as 'the scum of the earth', although the fact that he went on to say that the army turned them into 'fine fellows' is often forgotten. He held the common views of men of his class and time, expressed in pithy aphorisms. He believed in flogging and executions to maintain discipline, aware that coercion was a principal means of preventing the army from turning into a mob. But Wellington had a keen appreciation of the importance of the welfare of the rank and file, and on occasions his comments were tinged with gruff affection. Before Waterloo, asked about his chances of beating Napoleon, he pointed to a red-coated infantryman: 'it all depends on upon that article whether we shall do the business or not. Give me enough of it, and I am sure'.[35]

On the field of battle Wellington was a hands-on commander, sometimes excessively so. At Bussaco, he galloped up to Hill, an experienced and competent general, to give him unnecessarily detailed instructions. This incident underlines Wellington's disdain for allowing his subordinates genuine initiative, and his propensity for getting sucked into tactical detail. But Wellington made his command style work. Not the least of his genius was how he managed to micromanage without losing sight of the bigger picture. Wellington's army was small enough and compact enough for him to command from the front. Within a century the vast expansion of the size of armies and the area over which they operated had rendered this approach unworkable. While many of Wellington's attributes (his attention to logistics, his skill in managing coalitions, his fingertip feeling) are timeless, his highly personalised command style would sit uneasily with modern Western armed forces. Wellington was undoubtedly a military genius, but he was a genius of his time.

8

On the Offensive, 1811–1812

As Masséna's army retreated to Spain in March 1811, Wellington followed him cautiously. The pursuit was hampered by crossing a stretch of country that had been subjected to his own scorched-earth policy, and then picked over by the French, so his army was forced to halt to allow supplies to be brought up. Portugal was lost to the French, with the exception of the fortress of Almeida. However it was simply not possible for Wellington to follow up his success in clearing Portugal by driving the enemy from Spain. The French situation was too strong: Soult took the fortress of Badajoz on 10 March, so the two 'Keys of Spain' on the Spanish side of the frontier were now in French hands. If Masséna and Soult, overcoming personal rivalries and logistic problems, succeeded in bringing their forces together, the combined army would considerably outnumber the Anglo-Portuguese. Wellington was thus compelled to split his army. He held the bulk under his own command within striking distance of Cuidad Rodrigo, while 120 miles to the south, ten days march along poor roads, which were vulnerable to being interdicted, was Beresford's 20,000 men. Wellington spent some days in the south with Beresford in mid April supervising preparation for the siege of Badajoz.

On 3 May Masséna attempted to regain the initiative by lunging towards Almedia, blockaded by the British. The two armies clashed at Fuentes d'Oñoro. Fierce fighting erupted in the narrow streets. At a critical moment, Wellington personally committed three battalions, which drove the French out of the village. After spending 4 May regrouping, on 5 May Masséna sent three infantry divisions supported by a large body of cavalry to turn Wellington's southern flank. That his gambit almost succeeded owed much to that rare thing, a tactical mistake by Wellington. The British commander was aware what was afoot but, presumably through over confidence, he made inadequate provision to defend the largely open ground on his right. Wellington despatched the Light Division to extract the 7th Division and an epic, and ultimately successful, fighting retreat ensued. He also established a new flank, thus abandoning his only safe road back to Portugal. Wellington's risk this time paid off. The Anglo-Portuguese army stood firm, and Masséna broke off the battle. Wellington had won a tactical victory, and more importantly prevented the French from relieving Almeida.

Even the greatest generals sometimes make mistakes, but one of the marks of greatness is the ability to recognise and respond to mistakes in a timely and appropriate way. The battle was 'the most difficult I was ever concerned in', Wellington admitted candidly; 'If Boney had been there, we should have been beat'. But once it became all too clear that he had blundered, Wellington acted promptly to retrieve his error. After Fuentes d'Oñoro, Wellington 'remains the terror and admiration of the French army',

Gordon wrote after meeting French officers. 'They were all witnesses to his masterly change of position on the 5th, and which they were not able to prevent'. The French rated Wellington more highly than the Austrian Archduke Charles, who had defeated Napoleon at Aspern-Essling in 1809. 'They said the other day that their Emperor would not disdain to encounter him': high praise indeed.[36]

Fuentes d'Oñoro was followed by two setbacks. First, on the night of 10–11 May, the French garrison at Almeida evaded the investing force and escaped. Wellington was incandescent and fulminated that he could not trust his subordinates. A little later a battle was fought that showed that Wellington's sour comment, if exaggerated, was not entirely wide of the mark. On 16 May 1811 the village of Albuera became the scene of the bloodiest British battle of the Peninsular War. Beresford's Anglo-Spanish force came close to defeat before the situation was restored at the price of horrendous casualties. Wellington arrived a few days after the battle, and visited some wounded survivors. 'I am sorry to see so many of you here,' he told them. The reply from one old soldier was telling: 'If you had commanded us, my Lord, there wouldn't be so many of us here.' Wellington tried to encourage Beresford, but the latter had shown himself out of his depth as an independent commander. Yet Albuera, but not Fuentes d'Oñoro, was hailed as a victory in Britain. Wellington disliked the downbeat tone of Beresford's initial dispatch, telling an officer 'this won't do, write me down a victory' and helping in the redrafting. He saw that Beresford's 'whining report … would have driven the people in England mad'.

By spinning news this way, Wellington was maintaining the political momentum achieved by liberating Portugal. On 29 May, Liverpool wrote to Wellington giving him

> full discretion to undertake such operation as may be best calculated at that time to bring the war to a successful termination, and you will consider yourself therefore at liberty to employ the means necessary … to attain that important object.

At last, Wellington had the political backing he needed to campaign as he saw fit, without constantly looking over his shoulder at London. Victories are won at home as well as on the battlefield.[37]

This was not the end of Wellington's operations in 1811. Badajoz was once again besieged unsuccessfully. Ciudad Rodrigo was blockaded. In September Marshal Marmont, Masséna's replacement, advanced to resupply the fortress and during a week of manoeuvring and minor actions there was a possibility of a major battle. Wellington miscalculated, leaving his forces dispersed in the face of a numerically superior enemy. He partially redeemed himself by his calm generalship, but he was probably fortunate that Marmont decided not to launch a major attack. At El Bodón, (25 September) a small-scale French advance was repulsed, but two days later Wellington retreated to Portugal.

The campaign of 1811 demonstrated that the Peninsular War was stalemated. On the battlefield, it was possible to win convincing victories but the deadlock was at the operational (campaign) and strategic levels. The French could not unite their armies in the Peninsula to deal Wellington a decisive blow, partly because of the problems of feeding such a host, and because to do so would have been to abandon hard-won territory to the Spanish guerrillas and field armies, which showed impressive resilience in the face of constant defeat. Napoleon showed no sign of massively reinforcing his armies in Spain and taking command in person. For his part Wellington's army lacked the strength to undertake a major offensive and so he had no option but to continue with his Fabian methods. Wellington at this stage had to be an opportunist: to wait upon events, hoping that something would alter the situation in his favour. That 'something' was growing tension between France and Russia.

During 1811, relations between Napoleon and Czar Alexander deteriorated steadily. At root was growing Russian resistance to participating in the Continental System. Wellington's victories in the Peninsula, which were admired in Russia, played a role in keeping the anti-Napoleonic flame alight. In March 1812 a Russian envoy in Paris reported that French officers told him that, if Napoleon invaded, Russian strategy should seek to exhaust the enemy by avoiding battle, prolonging the campaign, and harrying the invaders: 'the system we should follow in this war is the one of which Fabius and indeed Lord Wellington offer the best examples'.[38] Napoleon began to assemble a new *Grande Armée* for a campaign in Russia, which included 27,000 men withdrawn from Spain. He accepted the advantage that this redeployment gave his enemies but refused to abandon the offensive in the Peninsula. Instead, Napoleon instructed Suchet to take the key fortress of Valencia, and stripped forces from other parts of Spain to reinforce him. Belatedly, the emperor made the sensible decision to appoint a supreme commander in Spain, albeit it was his militarily ineffectual brother, King Joseph. By removing troops to Russia and eastern Spain Napoleon shifted the odds in favour of Wellington, which perhaps indicates how little he thought of the British general. In any case, once Russia was defeated, any temporary Allied gains in Spain could be reversed. But for now Wellington held the initiative.

As early as May 1811 Wellington was anticipating that 'a war in the north' offered the opportunity to 'make Boney's situation in Spain this year not *a bed of roses*', and the British received much intelligence of French troops marching out of Spain. [39] The fact that the army in Portugal was receiving substantial reinforcements increased his confidence. At his prompting, Wellington's forthcoming campaign would be accompanied with operations by Spanish armies. Taking advantage of command of the sea, a British-led expedition from Sicily was to be mounted against the eastern coast of Spain, and units of Royal Marines deployed to cooperate with guerrillas in north-west Spain. Although these subsidiary operations achieved mixed success, they all contributed to tying down French troops that might otherwise have been used against Wellington.

Wellington's primary task was to capture the frontier fortresses. He moved against Ciudad Rodrigo early in

1812, beginning the siege on 8 January. By the 19th, the siege guns had made two substantial breaches in the walls, and, that night, parties of infantry stormed the city. Cuidad Rodrigo brought tangible reward to Wellington: he became a Spanish duke, taking the title of the recently captured city, as well as receiving a step up in the British nobility, being created the Earl of Wellington, with his pension doubling to £4,000 per annum. His heir thus became Viscount Douro. Ever mindful of wider issues, Wellington vetoed a suggestion that a new title be found for young Arthur: it might have been construed as an insult to his Portuguese soldiers.

With one of the keys of Spain firmly in his grasp, Wellington moved against the other, Badajoz. Wellington was well aware of the threat that Soult posed if he advanced north or if Marmont came south, or, worse, if the two French armies combined. Wellington remained at his headquarters at Frenenda to try to keep his opponents guessing as to his next move as long as possible, but in truth his next objective was obvious. But Soult was dilatory, and Marmont's freedom of action was restricted by Napoleon's attempts to command in Spain by remote control from far away. In the event Wellington was able to conduct operations against Badajoz unmolested by French field armies, although the possibility of their appearance understandably worried him, and he was prepared to fight a major battle. Badajoz was invested on 16 March 1812. Heavy rain and, as ever, an inadequate siege train hampered operations. When the siege was over, the heavy losses amongst the attacking infantry prompted Wellington to press the government to form a unit of sappers and miners. Nevertheless, the digging of siege lines proceeded steadily, with Wellington personally directing the work. By 6 April three breaches had been made in the walls, and after a personal reconnaissance, Wellington ordered that Badajoz would be stormed that evening at 10 p.m..

The 4th and Light Divisions assaulted the breaches, in Wellington's words, 'with the utmost intrepidity. But such was the nature of the obstacles prepared by the enemy ... and so determined their resistance, that our troops could not establish themselves within the place'. The losses were dreadful that night; in all, about 4,000 men fell, a third of the attacking strength. An eyewitness saw Wellington receiving yet more bad news that night: 'the jaw had fallen, and the face was of unusual length ... but still the expression of his face was firm'.[40] Disaster was redeemed by the unexpected success of a subsidiary assault, where men used scaling ladders to get onto the walls. Badajoz fell to Wellington's army. Then the fragile bonds that held the discipline of the army dissolved. In a berserk rage, the troops sacked Badajoz – a friendly city – without mercy. In the aftermath of the storming, Wellington no doubt experienced feelings of relief and achievement, but they were mixed with an unusual degree of grief (Picton came across him weeping) but also fury at the indiscipline of his men. Wellington 'fulminates orders', one of his aide-de-camp (ADC) recorded in his journal, 'and will hardly thank the troops, so angry is he'.[41] The sack of Badajoz went far beyond the bounds of what Wellington was prepared to tolerate, and it was a salutatory reminder to the iron disciplinarian of how an army could rapidly disintegrate into an armed mob.

With Ciudad Rodrigo and Badajoz in his grasp, Wellington was determined to strike at Marmont in central Spain, who posed the most immediate threat. Detaching Hill with 14,000 men to counter any move by Soult in the south (although Wellington suspected that Soult would unlikely to be keen to cooperate with his fellow marshal), by 17 June Wellington's army of 48,000 men had reached the city of Salamanca. This was the boldest advance into Spain that Wellington had attempted since the Talavera campaign three years before, and although it was not without risk, the potential gains were great – the capture of King Joseph Bonaparte's capital of Madrid, and perhaps even Burgos, a fortress strategically situated on the road to France. Before such ambitions could be translated into reality, Wellington needed to deal with Marmont's Army of Portugal. He had not entirely relinquished the 'cautious system', writing in late June to the new prime minister, Lord Liverpool that he had 'superiority of numbers ... [but] not so great as to render an action decisive of the result of the campaign'. Marmont too was being cautious, and both armies manoeuvred seeking an advantage. At San Christobal on 20 June Marmont declined to attack the Allied army, and although the moment seemed ripe, Wellington in turn decided, controversially, against taking the fight to the French. One of his staff commented that Wellington 'knows what it is right to do. He must to have attacked him given up the advantage of his position, and advanced ...

exposed to a very heavy fire … [I]f this army gets crippled very much it cannot continue the operation'.[42]

Marmont retreated some 40 miles to the Douro, followed by Wellington. There, the deadlock was renewed for two weeks. In mid July Wellington received information that King Joseph was advancing to support Marmont with a sizeable force. This blow was compounded by a sudden French advance, which forced the Allied army to retire. Yet again, Wellington could have been killed, captured or wounded, as he became involved in a cavalry action, and escaped with drawn sword. Then followed a remarkable episode as both armies headed towards Salamanca, sometimes marching in clear view of each other. With Wellington back where he started in the Christobal position on 21 July, there was no doubt that Marmont was winning the campaign. Wellington appeared to have little option but to abandon Salamanca and fall back, yet again, to the Portuguese frontier. There is a clue to his thinking in his frank admission to General Graham that 'Marmont ought to have given me a *pont d'or*, [a golden bridge, i.e. an opportunity to withdraw unmolested] and he would have made a handsome operation of it'.[43] By the time he wrote that, Wellington had won a battle that is widely regarded as his masterpiece.

The victory came about because in the delicate game of manoeuvre, Marmont had finally made a mistake. Near the twin hills of Los Arapiles, near Salamanca, on 22 July Marmont drove his forces forward in an attempt to outflank the city. As he did so Wellington saw that gaps had opened up between the French formations, so they could no longer support each other. Wellington had been waiting for the opportunity, and struck. Launching infantry and cavalry against the French, he won a crushing victory. If Spanish troops had not neglected to guard a vital river bridge, it would have been greater still. Salamanca gave Wellington, out-generalled at the operational level, his finest moment as an attacking battlefield commander. He recognised the opportunity that Marmont's error presented and seized it. Wellington was entitled to boast 'there never was an army so beaten in so short a time'.[44]

After Salamanca, Wellington's army entered Madrid on 12 August. Rewards followed. Wellington was created a marquess, and was appointed as commander-in chief of the Spanish army (although this was not to prove the advantage it might have seemed, and brought him into conflict with various factions in Spain). This was a time of worry for Wellington. The news of Marmont's disaster had a galvanising effect on some other French armies, and so Wellington was threatened by being overwhelmed by enemy forces converging on Madrid. So shortly after one of his finest moments as a general, Wellington endured two of his worst. First, he failed to bring the Army of Portugal (now commanded by General Clausel) to battle near Valladolid. Then he spent five weeks besieging Burgos. Lacking heavy guns, it was slow work, and attempts to storm the walls failed. Threatened by a French relief force, on 21 October Wellington raised the siege. Burgos marked the nadir of Wellington's siege-craft, and the failure was compounded by the nightmarish retreat that followed. He abandoned Madrid in the face of superior French forces advancing on the city, and fell back to Ciudad Rodrigo. With discipline coming under strain and 'croaking' among his troops, Wellington issued a circular letter, which caused much resentment, that claimed that regimental 'Officers lost all command over their men'.[45]

The retreat from Burgos was, as Wellington admitted, the 'worst scrape I ever was in'. His performance in 1812 was curiously patchy. Yet, back on the Portuguese frontier, blaming the Spaniards for his misfortunes, Wellington had reasons to be optimistic. Despite the political changes in London, he still had firm backing. In May Perceval was assassinated, and Wellington's ally Lord Liverpool replaced him as Prime Minister. In the Peninsula, the past year had seen, Wellington asserted to Liverpool, 'the most successful campaign in all its circumstances, and has produced for the cause more important results, than any campaign in which a British army has been engaged for the last century'.[46] Hyperbole aside, Wellington was fundamentally correct. In concentrating forces to oppose him, the French had been forced to abandon great tracts of land to the guerrillas, especially in southern Spain, and Cadiz was at last free from the besieging army. There was little prospect of the French reconquering the lost territory. King Joseph was back in Madrid, but his authority had been destroyed. Joseph's army would not be reinforced for Napoleon's expedition to Russia had ended in disaster, and France faced a major challenge from an emboldened Russia and Prussia. Wellington's army, reinforced from home and rested, would hold the strategic initiative in 1813. He intended to make full use of it.

9

Peninsular Endgame, 1813–1814

Concert-goers in Vienna in December 1813 were treated to a new piece by Ludwig van Beethoven entitled 'Wellington's Victory'. The fact that the great composer was so inspired by the Battle of Vitoria, fought earlier that year, indicates that Wellington's reputation had spread well beyond military and political circles. By the time Beethoven's composition was performed, Wellington and his army, having started the year at his base in Portugal, had advanced through Spain, crossed the Pyrenees and was firmly based on French soil.

What small chance the French armies in Spain had of recovering from the disasters of 1812 were undermined by Napoleon's continuing attempts to command from a distance. He underestimated the size of Wellington's force, and one of his senior officials dismissed the British general's 'constant and timid caution'.[47] Paris ordered troops to be sent to fight the guerrillas in northern Spain, reducing the forces that could face Wellington's army. Far from being cautiously timid, Wellington planned a campaign that would break decisively with his previous wariness. With Napoleon fighting a major campaign in Germany against the resurgent Russians and Prussians, he recognised that 'I cannot have a better opportunity' to force the French to battle. If the enemy lost, it 'must oblige him to withdraw altogether'.[48]

Wellington's preparations thus showed great ambition. Concerned about Marshal Suchet's force in eastern Spain, Wellington succeeded in getting an Allied force sent from Sicily. Although not very successful, along with guerrilla activity, this seaborne threat was to prevent Suchet from interfering with Wellington's operations. The Royal Navy gave Wellington great flexibility in his strategic options. He chose to move his supply bases from Portugal to northern Spain (the capture of the major port of Santander by an amphibious force in 1812 was critical to his strategy). The siege train was sent to Corunna, but kept on board ship. Until his army reached the north-eastern corner of Spain, Wellington's soldiers would be largely reliant on supplies that they could carry. Mobile, 'light and quick' methods were the order of the day, so that, for instance, heavy iron kettles were replaced by lighter tin vessels.

Wellington's preparations in the early months of 1813 were political as well as military. They included difficult negotiations in Portugal, which was showing signs of war-weariness. Handling the Spanish Cortes also took up much time and energy. A new, liberal constitution had been introduced in 1812. Naturally, Wellington was opposed: 'I wish that some of our reformers would go to Cadiz to see the benefit of a sovereign popular assembly … In truth there is no authority in the state'.[49]

The army finally struck camp on 13 May. Wellington accompanied Hill's corps, marching along the familiar road towards Salamanca. As he crossed the frontier into

Spain, he is said to have flourished his hat and declared, 'Farewell, Portugal! I shall never see you again!'[50] Wellington was keen to be noticed there by the enemy, because Hill's march was a subsidiary operation, part of a deception plan. The bulk of his forces were elsewhere, where they crossed the River Douro and advanced through the broken terrain of Trás-os-Montes in northern Portugal, an area usually avoided by armies. The route was previously reconnoitred, and the army was accompanied by a bridging train to allow the most direct route to be taken across rivers. Wellington's trademark thorough preparations and staff work smoothed the advance, but even so there were some shortages of food.

Wellington's strategic gambit paid off handsomely. His forces outflanked the French, leaving their dispersed forces helplessly behind as he drove into northern Spain. Hill's corps too had swung north, rather than heading for Madrid. With its communications route back to France in peril, King Joseph's army was forced into a demoralising retreat. Burgos, the rock upon which Wellington's wave had broken in 1812, was abandoned. With the exception of a cavalry action on 2 June, the early phase of the campaign did not witness much fighting. By 21 June, brilliant manoeuvres and hard marching had gained Wellington a potentially decisive advantage. On that day, near the town of Vitoria, he sought to capitalise on that advantage by destroying the French army in battle.

The French force of 60,000 at Vitoria was not in good shape. Joseph's army had been driven back from central Spain to within 70 miles of France, and had been joined by other French units (and still others were in the process of marching towards it). Three French divisions had been roughly handled shortly before the battle. The army had a tail of camp followers, including Spanish Bonapartists escaping from revengeful patriots. Joseph's chief of staff, Marshal Jourdan, was sick before the battle. This may explain why the French troops were poorly deployed, with little attempt to guard against anything but an attack from the west. This played into Wellington's hands. He planned a very ambitious manoeuvre, with 70,000 men in four columns attacking from different points. Hill's column (including a Spanish division) struck to the south, capturing and holding key high ground, which attracted a strong French force to this sector. To the north-east, the Light Division crossed over the River Zadorra on a bridge that was, amazingly, unguarded, and advanced on the French position. It is likely that Wellington intended these attacks to hold the French in place, while Dalhousie's column attacked from the north, and Graham's men emerged to the north of Vitoria to threaten the road back to France.

While Wellington's immensely testing plan did not succeed in its entirety – Graham's supposed sluggishness in the advance has been criticised, although not by Wellington – the end of the day saw the French army outflanked and routed, its baggage looted (to Wellington's extreme displeasure) and Napoleon's ambitions in Spain utterly destroyed. Wellington wrote to his brother Henry: 'I have the pleasure to inform you that we beat the French army commanded by the King in a general action near Vitoria yesterday having taken from them more than 120 pieces of cannon, all their ammunition, baggage, provisions, money &c. Our loss has not been severe.'[51] The prince received Jourdan's baton as a Marshal of France as a gift. Not to be outdone, he appointed Wellington a field marshal.

Since early June there had been an uneasy truce between the Prussian-Russian alliance and Napoleon. Far away in Germany, at a gathering of Allied monarchs and commanders, when Czar Alexander heard of the news of Vitoria he commanded the singing of a *Te Deum*. Negotiations with France broke down, and in mid August the war was renewed – with hitherto neutral Austria joining the Allies. Vitoria greatly strengthened Britain's hand in dealing with its allies, and may even have played a modest role in stiffening their resolve to renew the war.

In the wake of Vitoria Napoleon finally amalgamated the armies in Spain (with the exception of Suchet's) under one commander. He made a good choice in Nicholas Soult – a capable and aggressive general who restored the morale of his troops. With most of Spain lost, Marshal Soult was able to mass his forces against Wellington, who soon found himself on the defensive. On the coast, the fortress-port of San Sebastian was besieged by the Allies, while 40 miles away Pamplona, a key road junction, was blockaded. As long as these places remained in French hands, Wellington would find it very difficult to advance. With the army spread out along a wide front in mountainous terrain, Wellington, who preferred to hold all the threads in his own hands, was forced to trust the commanders on the spot.

Soult struck on 25 July, with French columns capturing the passes of Maya and Roncesvalles. The defence of both positions were mishandled by the local commanders. Matters were made worse by the failure to keep Wellington properly informed. Had the French capitalised on their success, and reached Pamplona, it would have placed the Allied army in a very dangerous position. As it was, the Allies fell back to Sorauen, the last possible place to fight a defensive battle before the French reached the walls of Pamplona. Wellington himself arrived to take command, and was greeted by heartfelt cheers from the common soldiers and sighs of relief from his officers. The battle that followed was a throwback to the earlier years of the Peninsular War, with French columns attacking British lines determinedly holding a ridgeline. The outcome of this 'fair *bludgeon* work', as Wellington called it, was utterly predictable. By the middle of the first week of August, Soult's army was back where it had started, its offensive at an end. Nonetheless, it had been an unpleasant shock to Wellington, who was privately scathing about his subordinates. 'It is a great disadvantage,' he told Lord Liverpool, when the 'Commander-in-Chief must be absent ... there is nothing I dislike so much as these extended operations, which I cannot direct myself.'[52]

What to do next weighed heavily on Wellington's mind in the late summer of 1813. An attempt to get through the Pyrenees to invade France was an obvious option, but much depended on the state of the hostilities between Napoleon and the anti-French coalition in central Europe. There was a risk that a compromise peace, or even a decisive French victory, would lead to large forces being diverted to face Wellington. Marshal Suchet's army in Catalonia was also a concern, and Wellington contemplated moving to eliminate the threat to his eastern flank. Until San Sebastian fell, his hands were tied. The first assault, launched on 25 July, was a failure. General Graham was in charge, and, true to type, an observer witnessed Wellington's agitation while he waited for news, unable directly to influence events. San Sebastian fell at the second attempt, on 31 August. Wellington was now free to cross the Bidassoa, the river that separated Spain from France, and set the army to battle its way over the passes of the Pyrenees. Although under pressure from press and politicians in Britain, even at this stage he had not finally decided on a full-scale invasion of France, but was awaiting the outcome of events in Germany.

The next phase of Wellington's campaign has a very modern feel. Using the principles of what today would be called 'operational art', like a skilful chess player Wellington planned several moves ahead, seeking to capture an objective to make the next advance possible. This stepping-stones approach was not intended, in the short-term, to bring about a decisive battle in this difficult terrain, but rather, in Huw Davies' words, to 'force the French to a more traditional battlefield where [he could fight a] conventional battle'.[53] These operations rate among Wellington's finest military achievements.

The Allied army attacked across the Bidassoa on 7 October. It was a tough fight, as the banks of the river were fortified by the defenders, but by the end of the day Wellington's men became the first enemy army to set foot on French territory since the days of the Revolutionary

War. Prestige was accompanied by tactical advantages. With the fall of Pamplona, the eastern bastion of the French position, on 31 October, Wellington's hand was strengthened. Whatever his ultimate objective, Wellington was aware of the danger of his army being stuck in the mountains in a Pyrenean winter. On 10 November Wellington struck across the River Nivelle and drove the French back. News of Napoleon's calamitous defeat at the Battle of Nations at Leipzig in mid October had reached both armies on the day before the attack, but even then Wellington was cautious, fearing that peace might be patched up in Germany. Wellington crossed the Nive on 10 December, defeating a French counterattack in the process. On 12 December, Hill won a defensive victory at St Pierre, almost at the gates of Bayonne. Then a combination of bad weather and Wellington's waiting upon events brought campaigning to a halt.

While he was conducting the Pyrenees campaign, Wellington was also dealing with the thousand and one other matters that demanded his attention. His difficult relations with the Spanish authorities came to a head in November 1813 when Wellington sent a furious letter to London demanding that the British army should return home unless the Spanish made major concessions. Not surprisingly, this demand fell on deaf ears. This incident tells us much about the stress that Wellington was experiencing at this time, and reflects poorly on his judgement as a coalition commander. His attitude to the Spanish troops under his immediate command were ambivalent. During the battle of St Marcial in August, Wellington paid a Spanish force a compliment by refusing to send British reinforcements, so they could claim the victory unaided. But as the army pushed on into France, his Spaniards became a liability. On 1 November Wellington issued a proclamation promising that civilians would not be molested. But as he wrote privately, '[W]ithout pay and food', the Spanish soldiery 'must plunder; and ... ruin us all'. He had no wish to stir up a French guerrilla movement. 'I prefer to have a small army that will obey my orders, and preserve discipline,' he informed a Spanish general, 'to a large one that is disobedient'.[54]

With Napoleon desperately fending off overwhelming Allied forces in eastern France, Wellington's advance resumed in mid February 1814. The end was in sight: as his army marched through south-west France, Wellington was struck by the enthusiasm for a restoration of the Bourbon monarchy, and wrongly assumed that the rest of the country felt that way. In winning the Battle of Orthez on 27 February Wellington was badly bruised by a spent musket ball. Subsequently Bordeaux capitulated without a fight. Wellington's final victory of the Peninsular War was won outside Toulouse on 10 April. The armies fought needlessly. Napoleon had abdicated four days earlier, but the news only reached Wellington in Toulouse on 12 April. That evening, at dinner, he drank the health of the new French monarch, Louis XVIII. His dinner guests promptly toasted Wellington himself – as the liberator of Spain, liberator of Portugal, liberator of Europe – and cheered him to the echo. Embarrassed, Lord Wellington 'bowed, confused, and immediately called for coffee'.[55]

10

Waterloo, 1815

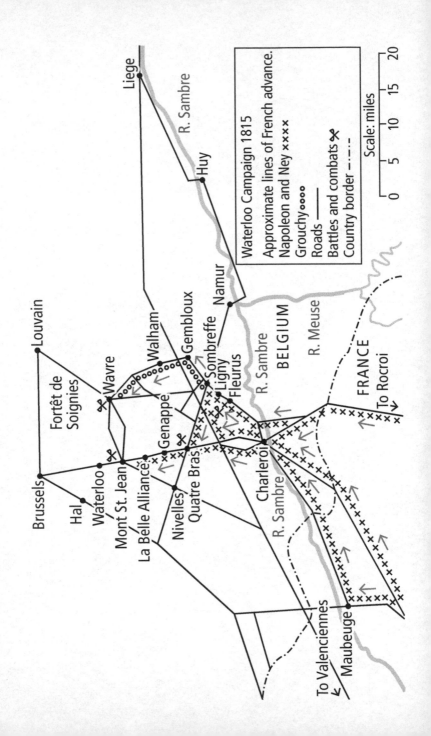

Wellington was handsomely rewarded for his victory in the Peninsula War with a dukedom and £400,000. His return to Britain was marked by adulation – cheering crowds, dinners, a thanksgiving service at St Paul's Cathedral – all of which was rather different to his previous visit, in 1809, in the aftermath of Cintra. Appointed as the British ambassador to France, Wellington went to Paris. This was not the most tactful of appointments, and in February 1815 he replaced Castlereagh as the British representative in Vienna, where the great powers were seeking to reorder Europe. Britain was alarmed by the territorial ambitions of Prussia, which was backed by the Czar, and signed a secret treaty with Austria and France to resist them. War between the erstwhile allies seemed possible. Then, on 7 March, news reached Vienna that changed everything. Napoleon had escaped from exile on Elba and had landed in France. On 20 March the Corsican Ogre was back in Paris.

Although Napoleon had protested his peaceful intentions, the great powers proclaimed him an outlaw. War was inevitable, and Belgium – now united with the Netherlands – was very likely the scene of the next campaign. Britain had gone to war in 1793 largely because of the threat to its security should Belgium fall into hostile hands, and was to go to war with another enemy in 1914 for the same reason. Although Czar Alexander told Wellington that 'It is up to you to save the world again',[56] it was also British self-interest that sent the Duke to take command of the ramshackle army in Belgium. In the long term, the strategic auspices were good for the Allies. Large Austrian and Russian forces were being mobilised and beginning to march across Europe. The immediate picture was not so bright. Wellington's Peninsular army had been dispersed, with some troops sent off to North America to fight the United States in the so-called 'War of 1812'. The British battalions in Belgium tended to be filled with green troops. Britons were in any case in a minority among the Dutch-Belgians, and troops from a variety of minor German states. Some of these had previously fought for France, and their loyalty was in doubt. Wellington took over command from the 24-year-old Prince of Orange, the son of the King of the Netherlands. Wellington set to work to make the best of his army, mixing up British and non-British units and veterans and raw troops. One of Wellington's most notorious remarks, that he had 'an infamous army', dates from this period and must be seen in this context.[57]

Once again, Wellington was to be involved in coalition warfare. Much would depend on how effectively he could work with the Prussian army under 72-year-old Field Marshal Gebhard von Blücher. Wellington's army's lines of communications led back to the Channel ports, but Prussian supply lines went back to Germany. Napoleon's strategy appeared obvious: to seek to keep the two armies divided while destroying each enemy in turn. If Blücher and Wellington succeeded in uniting their armies, they would outnumber him. But Wellington could not rely on the greatest soldier of the age doing the obvious. Unlike in Spain, the Duke lacked reliable intelligence from friendly locals and guerrillas, and he had to plan for a French move around the flank of the Anglo-Dutch army to cut it off from the Channel ports. Wellington was not afraid of Napoleon, but he was understandably cautious. As 1940 was to show, British generals operating in Flanders have to have one eye on the coast, and this is a potential weakness that a shrewd enemy can exploit. Napoleon held the initiative, and Wellington was forced to wait until his adversary showed his hand.

On the night of 15 June 1815 the Duke was at the Duchess of Richmond's ball in Brussels – a shrewd move, which calmed civilian nerves - as were most of his leading subordinates. It was there that he learned that Napoleon was not seeking to outflank the Anglo-Dutch army. Wellington's reaction was to bark, 'Napoleon has humbugged me, by God; he has gained twenty-four hours march on me', and to order his forces to march to the crossroads at Quatre Bras. At that moment there was no more vital ground anywhere in Europe. The road east went to the village of Ligny, where Blücher's army was encamped. There Napoleon himself faced Blücher, while Marshal Ney marched on Quatre Bras. If Ney could swiftly occupy the crossroads, he could prevent Wellington from supporting Blücher while sending forces against the Prussian flank and rear as Napoleon attacked frontally.

Wellington's sluggish start to the campaign has been seen as a Machiavellian attempt to let the Prussians bear the brunt of the French attack. A simpler solution fits the evidence much better. Wellington had made the wrong call and was surprised by Napoleon. Certainly the Duke knew how vital Blücher's support would be, and it was simply not in his interest for the Prussian to be beaten.

Wellington's situation was exacerbated by his failure to recognise the importance of Quatre Bras. Luckily the Dutch commander on the spot ignored orders and so the key crossroads was occupied when the French arrived. Uncharacteristically, Wellington retrospectively sanctioned this defiance of his wishes. On 16 June Ney was slow to attack, perhaps fearing, as in the Peninsula, that Wellington had concealed many more troops than were visible. This combination of initial French hesitation and subsequent hard fighting bought time for reinforcements to arrive from Brussels, which Wellington deftly fed into battle on the basis of just enough, just in time. At the end of a day's heavy fighting the Allies still held the crossroads at Quatre Bras. At Ligny Blücher was defeated and pushed back, although his army was substantially intact. It seems that Wellington had hoped to send troops to aid the Prussians 'providing I am not attacked myself' and had told Blücher so when they met that morning, but the fierceness of the fight at Quatre Bras meant that was not possible.[58] Wellington had tied down a considerable number of enemy troops that could have proved decisive at Ligny, but the key factor was the misuse of a French corps which spent the day marching and counter-marching between the two battlefields, when it might have proved decisive on either. The two days of 15 and 16 June 1815 are not numbered among Wellington's finest.

In 1814 the Duke had noted the defensive possibilities of a low ridge near the town of Waterloo. It was to this ridge at Mont-Saint-Jean to which his army retreated on 17 June. There he determined to give battle, if the Prussians would support him. General Gneisenau, Blücher's powerful chief of staff, in the absence of his injured boss, took the vital decision to retreat north rather than east from Ligny, thus holding out the possibility of aiding Wellington. Early on the 18th, Wellington was informed that the Prussians would indeed march to his aid. Given the state of his army, Wellington had no option but to fight a defensive battle, clinging to the ridge until the Prussians arrived.

Wellington feared a 'Napoleonic' sweep around his western flank, and so sensibly left troops beyond the battlefield at Hals. But Napoleon, underestimating his opponent, opted for a frontal assault. Wellington, while no doubt relieved, was also a little disappointed: 'Damn the fellow, he is a mere pounder after all'.[59] Following an artillery bombardment, the French launched massive infantry columns against the ridge. Lying down on the reverse slope, the artillery did little damage but the sheer weight of the columns almost broke the Allied line before Lord Uxbridge released a brilliantly timed cavalry charge that swept the French back. The cavalry then got out of hand and were virtually destroyed by a French counter-charge. What followed showed that Wellington was a lucky general. The French launched unsupported cavalry attacks against the Allied infantry in square. Had the French combined infantry and horse artillery with the cavalry, Wellington probably would have been defeated. Similarly, had Grouchy's detached force reinforced Napoleon, this too could have been decisive. Later still, had the French capitalised on their capture of La Haye Sainte, a farmhouse in front of the British centre, Napoleon could have won the battle. But by that stage, in the late afternoon, the Prussians were advancing dangerously close to the French flank. French troops were sent against Blücher rather than Wellington. The crisis passed.

The circumstances of Waterloo gave Wellington no scope for brilliant manoeuvre, but he did shine as the commander of a static army. Thus, early on, he recognised the French attack against the farm of Hougoumont as a diversion, and dribbled just enough reinforcements to keep the position safe. He was not afraid to micromanage. When he saw the roof was alight, the Duke sent a message direct to the defenders: 'keep your Men in those parts to which the fire does not reach'. He mostly stationed himself by a tree near the centre of his position, but frequently rode up and down a three-quarter-of-a-mile stretch of the battle line. In doing so, he took the pulse of the battle, ordering units forward, and encouraging his men, sometimes by a few words but more importantly by his presence. In doing so, Wellington exposed himself to danger. More than once he took shelter in a square from charging French cavalry. After the battle Wellington declared that, 'The finger of Providence was upon me, and I escaped unhurt'. With that fingertip feeling for battle, the Duke was on the spot when Napoleon threw in his Imperial Guard in a final attempt to snatch victory. Wellington calmly gave orders to the British Guards, who opened fire and set in train the hitherto unthinkable – the sight of Napoleon's elite running away. Dutch troops and the 52nd Light Infantry completed the rout. It was the end. With the Prussians advancing to their flank and rear, the brittle morale of Napoleon's army shattered. Wellington thrice waved his bicorn hat towards the French, and his army swept forward to complete the victory.[60]

Waterloo was, in Wellington's words, 'a near-run thing'. 'It was the most desperate business I was ever in,' he wrote to his brother on the following day, '& was never so near beat'. In later years he would try to downplay the importance of the role of the Prussians, but on 18 June 1815 he had no such illusions. At around 5.45 p.m. he is said to have uttered, 'Night or the Prussians must come'. This sounds suspiciously melodramatic and un-Wellingtonian, but the sentiment is accurate and in his dispatch he handsomely acknowledged the importance of Blücher's army in the victory. Waterloo was not Wellington's greatest battle in a technical military sense – it was just not that sort of battle – but he demonstrated iron resolve, inspirational leadership, and tactical mastery.[61]

It was a victory dearly bought. There were 50,000 casualties at Waterloo, as many as 17,000 of which were from Wellington's army. Wellington's friends and colleagues were among the killed and maimed. 'I hope to God that I have fought my last battle,' he told a female confidant. 'It is a bad thing to be always fighting'.[62]

11

After Waterloo

As soldier, the Duke of Wellington was a giant. His post-Waterloo career as a politician does not warrant such an accolade. That is not to say he was a bad politician. Wellington crossed the invisible border from 'politician' to 'statesman', and recent historians have reassessed and to some extent refurbished his reputation in government. He was undoubtedly a significant politician, and had some successes. No one, however, would include Wellington in a list of the greatest British Prime Ministers. When assessing his genius, his long career as a domestic politician inevitably appears as but a coda to his time as a soldier.

After three years as the commander-in-chief of the Allied army of occupation in France, in December 1818 Wellington took up a post in the Cabinet as Master General of the Ordnance. In January 1828 the Duke became Prime Minster. He took up the portfolio through a sense of duty rather than ambition or personal preference, and found the adjustment from leading a great army to leading a government difficult. As a general, he recalled nostalgically, 'I assembled my officers and laid down my plan, and it was carried into effect without any more words'.[63] As Prime Minister he could not simply give orders, but had to deal with egos, factions and ambitions, untainted by discipline.

In the matter of Catholic emancipation (the drive to grant political rights to Roman Catholics) Wellington showed a strong streak of pragmatism. As a reactionary Tory, a product of the Irish Protestant Ascendency, he might have been expected to resist the measure to the bitter end. However, alarmed by the prospect of disorder, and even rebellion, in Ireland, Wellington concluded that reform was the only option. He became the target of virulent anti-Catholic prejudice. This culminated in a duel between Wellington and Lord Winchilsea, who had accused him of planning 'the introduction of Popery in every department of the State'.[64] Neither men fired to kill. Catholic emancipation passed into law in April 1829. This was Wellington's greatest achievement as a domestic politician, and paradoxically ensured that this unbending Tory deserves honourable mention in any list of progressive actions that have shaped modern Britain.

Wellington took a very different stance on the next major political issue, the campaign for political reform. He resisted the clamour for abolition of rotten boroughs and the enfranchisement of the growing industrial centres; in short, he opposed the introduction of a limited measure of democracy. The pragmatism Wellington had showed over Catholic emancipation deserted him, and with pressure mounting, he was forced to resign as Prime Minister in November 1832. Out of office, Wellington continued to be vociferous in opposition to reform, and his popularity reached its nadir. His nickname of 'the Iron Duke' dates from this period, which initially was used pejoratively. Radicals feared that Wellington might turn out to be a modern Cromwell, using the army to destroy the constitution. The windows of his London home, Aspley House, were broken by the mob, and on Waterloo Day 1832 Wellington was threatened by a hostile crowd. Thus far the Duke's popular reputation had fallen. It was to recover.

Politics never quite relinquished its grip on Wellington. He acted as caretaker Prime Minister for three weeks in 1834, remarkably combining this post with the other senior positions in the Cabinet. This meant that the incoming Prime Minister, Sir Robert Peel, who was returning from overseas, could create a ministry from scratch. This, at least in theory, made Wellington the most powerful British politician since Cromwell. Twelve years later, in 1846, the 77-year-old Wellington made an influential speech in favour of the repeal of the Corn Laws, which helped sway the Lords to pass one of the most crucial pieces of legislation that came before a mid-nineteenth-century parliament.

Running parallel with his political career was Wellington's role as an army administrator. He was commander-in-chief of the army in 1827–28 and from 1842 until his death, and always had substantial influence on military affairs. His reactionary views have been blamed for the state of the army that was sent to the Crimea in 1854, two years after his death. This is only partially true: occasionally, as in the introduction of a rifled musket for the army as a whole, he would support innovation. Numerous reforms did take place in the army during Wellington's lifetime, albeit often in the teeth of the great man's opposition. Nonetheless, he succeeded in placing a brake on some important changes, including the introduction of short-term enlistments to help recruiting and create a manpower reserve.

Kitty, Wellington's duchess, died in 1831. The marriage had been no happier in its latter years than earlier. She was desperate to please him, but in his eyes she could do little right. All the more painful for Kitty was that Wellington gave his affection to other women in the form of affairs and close platonic friendships. Although he could be very good with children, Wellington was a distant father to his own. His temper was not improved by losing the hearing in one ear, as the result of medical treatment that went badly wrong. Left to himself, Wellington preferred a simple life, but he was rarely left to himself. Never able to refuse to carry out what he conceived as his duty, even while he complained about the burden, at various times he was chancellor of University the Oxford, colonel of several regiments, and, in the last ten years of his life, commander-in-chief of the army. Wellington's death, on 14 September 1852, prompted the young Queen Victoria to write that 'this great and immortal man belongs now to History'.[65]

12

Legacy and Assessment

As a general, Wellington had the mark of 'genius':

> transcendent common sense, the rare power ... of
> seeing things as they are ... [geniuses can] see clearly
> at a glance many things that puzzle other men. Seeing
> clearly they can decide to act promptly, and deciding
> promptly they can act immediately.[66]

As a general, who are Wellington's peers? Napoleon
was another soldier who was similarly gifted, but unlike
Wellington, he was ultimately unsuccessful in war. As
Wellington never had Napoleon's political power and
authority, one is not truly comparing like with like. Even
when generalship is treated more narrowly, as a technical
exercise of strategy, operations and tactics, accurate
comparisons are difficult. Wellington never commanded
anything the size of Napoleon's *Grande Armée* of 1812, or
conducted operations across a theatre as large as Russia.
It is also difficult to make meaningful comparisons across
different periods of military history. By the late nineteenth
century technology and the emergence of general staffs
had altered the conduct of war quite markedly.

Yet some things about the practice of command have not
changed much over the years. Wellington, like most highly

successful battlefield commanders could 'read' the strengths and weaknesses of a piece of terrain, and the use that the enemy had made of it. His genius in choosing defensive positions was almost proverbial, but battles such as Assaye and Vitoria show that Wellington was equally comfortable with offensive operations. He shared with Napoleon and Robert E. Lee inherent aggressiveness, although this was masked by circumstances of the Peninsula, which often forced him onto the defensive. Wellington was skilled in what today would be called operational art, and he had a highly developed feel for the politics of command. A keen appreciation of the importance of logistics and intelligence; an inspiring battlefield leader; a shrewd grasp of strategy and coalition warfare – the list of Wellington's military virtues goes on and on. Even his faults, such as his unwillingness to delegate and his discouragement of initiative, were not so great as to reduce his overall performance as a commander. Among British generals, only the Duke of Marlborough can really be compared to Wellington. The conditions of twentieth century total war were just too different to make comparisons with the likes of Haig and Montgomery have much meaning, although Bill Slim's conduct of operations in Burma suggest that he had a number of Wellington's qualities.

Nelson was Wellington's only rival as an embodiment of national pride during his lifetime. The admiral was a very different type of hero, a self-publicising and vain man who thrived on adulation. Wellington, by contrast, despised the masses. As heroes go, Nelson had the advantage of dying in battle, while Wellington had a long political career ahead of him which temporarily dented his popularity. Nelson was a genuinely popular hero, while the cult of Wellington was promoted by the establishment. The Duke was a partisan figure. The radical Jeremy Bentham in 1817 declared that, 'Waterloo will one day be pointed to by the historian as the grave, not only of French but of English liberties'. [67] Towards the end of his life, Wellington began to be treated as being above politics, a national figure around whom all could unite. This was a process that accelerated after his death, his post-1815 political career being downplayed as an embarrassment.

Wellington is a global figure, an embodiment of empire. He gave his name to the capital of New Zealand, while there are Waterloos in (among other places) Britain, Canada, Australia, USA and Sierra Leone. Salamanca Place in Hobart, Tasmania is representative of the hundreds, perhaps thousands, of streets across the old British Empire named after Wellington or his battles. Unlike many long-dead generals and politicians who gave their names to pubs and streets, today people still know Wellington. He is played by actors in television series, features in popular novels and is the subject of TV documentaries. There are a select band of historical 'giants' who have a place in the modern British mental landscape. They include Shakespeare, Nelson, Churchill ... and Wellington.

Acknowledgements

In the Introduction I listed the authors that have influenced my thinking on Wellington; I have found the work of Rory Muir and Huw Davies particularly helpful. The format of the series, which reduces scholarly apparatus to a minimum, means that I cannot acknowledge my scholarly debts to all these authors as directly as I would have wished. I hope that this will suffice as an apology. Anyone wishing to go further into the subject should read their work. I am very grateful to Dr Huw Davies who read the initial manuscript, although any mistakes that remain are my fault, not his. I am also indebted to Tony Morris, who commissioned this book, and my editor, Sophie Bradshaw.

Notes

1 Clausewitz, Karl von, M. Howard and P. Paret (eds), *On War* (Princeton University Press, 1976), p.100.

2 Connolly, S.J., 'Eighteenth Century Ireland: Colony or *ancien régime*?' in Boyce, D. George, and O'Day, Alan (eds), *The Making of Modern Irish History* (Routledge, 1996), p.26.

3 Butler, Iris, *The Eldest Brother: The Marquess Wellesley 1760–1842* (Hodder and Stoughton, 1973), pp.215–16.

4 Longford, Elizabeth, *Wellington: The Years of the Sword* (Panther, 1972), p.114.

5 Longford, pp.44, 46.

6 Longford, p.47.

7 Thomas, R.N.W., 'Wellington in the Low Countries, 1794–1795', *International History Review*, 11, 1, (1989) p.18.

8 Thomas, p.20.

9 Stanhope, P.H., *Notes of Conversations with the Duke of Wellington* (John Murray, 1888), p.182.

10 Severn, John, *Architects of Empire: The Duke of Wellington and his Brothers* (University of Oklahoma Press, 2007), p.69.

11 Holmes, Richard, *Wellington: The Iron Duke* (HarperCollins, 2003), p.49.

12 Davies, Huw J., *Wellington's Wars* (Yale University Press, 2012), p.34.

13 Holmes, p.81.

14 Muir, Rory, *Wellington: The Path to Victory, 1769-1814* (Yale University Press, 2013), p.141.

15 Pool, Bernard (ed.), *The Croker Papers 1808–1857* (Barnes & Noble, 1967), pp.164–5.

16 Haythornthwaite, Philip, *Wellington: The Iron Duke* (Potomac, 2007), p.20.

17 Gurwood, John (ed.), *The Dispatches of Field Marshal The Duke of Wellington* [hereafter, WD], Vol. III (Cambridge University Press, 2010), pp.181–3.

18 Longford, p.442.

19 Haythornthwaite, p.33.

20 Holmes, p.142.

21 Gleig, George, *The Life of Arthur, Duke of Wellington* (Longmans, 1865), pp.110–11.

22 Stanhope, pp.20, 162–3.

23 Wellington to William Wellesley-Pole, 6 April 1810, in Brett-James, Anthony, *Wellington at War 1794–1815* (Macmillan, 1961), p.190.

24 Wellington to Liverpool, 28 November 1809 and 2 April 1810, in *WD*, III, pp.610, 812.

25 Oman, Charles, *A History of the Peninsular War*, Vol. III, (Greenhill, 1996), p.266.

26 Wellington to Wellesley-Pole, 8 December 1810, in Brett-James, p.202.

27 Pool, *Croker Papers*, p.237.

28 Wellington to Hill, 18 June 1812, *WD*, V, p.712.

29 Muir, Rory (ed.). *At Wellington's Right Hand: The Letters of Lieutenant-Colonel Sir Alexander Gordon 1808–1815* (Sutton for Army Records Society, 2003), p.230.

30 Hathaway, Eileen (ed.), *A True Soldier Gentleman: The Memoirs of Lt. John Cooke 1791–1813* (Swanage: Shinglepicker, 2000), p.181.

31 Gordon to Lord Aberdeen, 27 November 1811, in Muir, *Right Hand*, p.268; Dr Hume quoted in Muir, *Right Hand*, p.405.

32 Wellington to Liverpool, 15 May 1811, *WD*, V, p.21.

33 Hibbert, Christopher (ed.), *Captain Gronow* (Kyle Cathie, 1991), p.129; Monick, Stanley (ed.), *Douglas's Tale of the Peninsula and Waterloo* (Leo Cooper, 1997), pp.43–4.

34 Forrest, Alan, *Waterloo* (Oxford University Press, 2015), p.87.

35 Stanhope, p.18; Longford, p.488.

36 Glover, Michael, *The Peninsular War 1807-1814: A Concise History* (1974), p.155; Muir, *Right Hand*, p.424.

37 Longford, p.320; Wellington to Beresford, 19 May 1811, *WD*, V, p.25; Moon, Joshua, *Wellington's Two-Front War* (University of Oklahoma Press, 2001), p.97.

38 Lieven, Dominic, *Russia against Napoleon* (Penguin, 2010), p.85.

39 Brett-James, p.215.

40 Wellington to Liverpool, 7 April 1812, *WD*, V, p.572; Muir, *Path*, p.453.

41 Longford, p.337.

42 Wellington to Liverpool, 25 June 1812, *WD*, V, p.722; Glover, Michael, *Wellington as Military Commander* (1973), pp.124–5.

43 Wellington to Graham, 25 July 1812, *WD*, V, p.759.

44 Wellington to Bathurst, 24 July 1812, *WD*, V, p.758.

45 28 Nov. 1812, in Brett-James, p.252.

46 Holmes, pp.170–1; Wellington to Liverpool, 23 Nov. 1812, *WD*, VI p.174.

47 Glover, *Peninsular*, p.227.

48 Glover, *Peninsular*, p.228.

49 Wellington to Bathhurst, 27 January 1813, *WD*, VI, pp.256–7.

50 Esdaile, Charles, *The Peninsular War* (Penguin, 2003), p.443.

51 Wellington to Henry Wellesley, 22 June 1813, *WD*, VI, p.544.

52 Wellington to Bentinck, 5 August 1813, Wellington to Liverpool, 4 August 1813, *WD*, VI, pp.654, 649.

53 Davies, p.192.

54 Haythornthwaite, p.66.

55 Muir, *Path*, p.584.

56 Longford, p.474.

57 Wellington to Stewart, 8 May 1815, *WD*, VIII, p.67.

58 Bassford, Christopher, Moran, Daniel, and Gregory Pedlow, *On Waterloo: Clausewitz, Wellington and the Campaign of* 1815 (Clausewitz.Com, 2010), pp.277–8.

59 Longford, p.564.

60 Muir, Rory, *Wellington: Waterloo and the Fortunes of Peace 1815–1852* (Yale University Press, 2015), p.64; Longford, *Sword*, p.590.

61 Muir, *Waterloo*, p.80; Longford, p.569.

62 Longford, p.591.

63 Haythornthwaite, p.87.

64 Haythornthwaite, p.89.

65 David, Saul, *Victoria's Wars* (Penguin, 2007), p.150.

66 Fortescue, John, *Wellington* (Williams and Norgate, 1925), p.210.

67 Forest, p.126.

Timeline

1769	1 May (probable date): Birth of Arthur Wesley
1787	Commissioned into 73rd Highlanders
1790	Elected to Irish Parliament
1793	September: Buys lieutenant colonelcy in 33rd Foot
1794	15 September: Sees action for first time (at Boxtel)
1797	February: Arrives in India
1798	May: Changes spelling of surname to 'Wellesley'
1799	5/6 April: Action at Sultanpettah Topi
1800	10 September: Defeats Dhoondiah
1803	23 September: Battle of Assaye
1805	September: Returns to Britain
1806	April: Marries Catherine 'Kitty' Pakenham
1807	April: Appointed Chief Secretary for Ireland
	August–September: Denmark campaign
1808	17 and 21 August: Battles of Roliça and Vimeiro, followed by Convention of Cintra
1809	22 April: Takes command in Portugal
	12 May: Battle of Oporto
	27 July: Battle of Talavera
	26 August: Created Viscount Wellington of Talavera and Wellington

1810	27 September: Battle of Bussaco
	10 October: Army completes retirement
	inside Lines of Torres Vedras
1811	March: Masséna's French army retreats from
	Lines of Torres Vedras
	3–5 May: Battle of Fuentes D'Oñoro
	16 May: Battle of Albuera
1812	19 January: Storming and capture of Ciudad
	Rodrigo
	6 April: Storming and capture of Badajoz
	22 July: Battle of Salamanca
	12 August: Entry into Madrid
	21 October: Siege of Burgos abandoned
1813	21 June: Battle of Vitoria
	28 July–1 August: Battle of Sorauen
	7 October: Army crosses River Bidassoa into
	France
	10 November: Battle of the Nivelle
	9-10 December: Battle of the Nive
1814	27 February: Battle of Orthez
	6 April: Napoleon abdicates as emperor
	10 April: Battle of Toulouse
	3 May: Created Duke of Wellington
	5 July: Appointed ambassador to France
1815	3 February: Arrives at Congress of Vienna as
	British representative
	20 March: Having returned from exile on
	Elba, Napoleon enters Paris
	16 June: Battle of Quatre Bras
	18 June: Battle of Waterloo

1818	26 December: Appointed Master-General of the Ordnance
1827	Becomes commander-in-chief of army in January, resigns in April, reappointed in August
1828	9 January: Becomes Prime Minister and resigns as commander-in-chief
1830	16 November: Resigns as Prime Minister
1834	November–December: Caretaker Prime Minister
1842	15 August: Resumes post of commander-in-chief of army
1852	14 September: Dies at Walmer Castle

Further Reading

Davies, Huw J., *Wellington's Wars* (2012)

Esdaile, Charles (ed.), *The Duke of Wellington: Military Despatches* (2014)

Esdaile, Charles, *The Peninsular War* (2003)

Gleig, George, *The Life of Arthur, Duke of Wellington* (1865)

Glover, Michael, *The Peninsular War 1807–1814: A Concise History* (1974)

Glover, Michael, *Wellington as Military Commander* (1973)

Griffith, Paddy (ed.), *Wellington: Commander* (1985)

Griffith, Paddy (ed.), *A History of the Peninsular War Vol. IX: Modern Studies of the War in Spain and Portugal, 1808–14* (1999)

Guedalla, Philip, *The Duke* (1940)

Gurwood, John (ed.), *The Dispatches of Field Marshal The Duke of Wellington*, 8 volumes (2010)

Hall, Christopher D., *Wellington's Navy: Sea Power and the Peninsular War 1807–1814* (2004)

Haythornthwaite, Philip, *Wellington: The Iron Duke* (2007)

Holmes, Richard, *Wellington: The Iron Duke* (2003)

Longford, Elizabeth, *Wellington: Pillar of State* (1972)

Longford, Elizabeth, *Wellington: The Years of the Sword* (1969)

Muir, Rory, *Wellington: The Path to Victory, 1769-1814* (2013)

Muir, Rory, *Wellington: Waterloo and the Fortunes of Peace 1815-1852* (2015)

Myatt, Frederick, *British Sieges of the Peninsular War* (2008)

Oman, Charles, *A History of the Peninsular War*, 7 volumes (1995-97)

Severn, John, *Architects of Empire: The Duke of Wellington and his Brothers* (2007)

Weller, Jac, *On Wellington: The Duke and his Art of War* (1998)

Websites

http://www.lifeofwellington.co.uk/ (supports Rory Muir's biography)

http://www.napoleon-series.org/

pocket GIANTS

A series about people who changed the world –
and why they matter.

Series Editor – Tony Morris

www.thehistorypress.co.uk